7 Continents

9 Lives

Fay Chiang

Bowery Books
Bowery Poetry Series #8

YBK Publishers
New York

Please direct all inquiries to: Editors, Bowery Books, 310 Bowery, New York, NY 10012

Bowery Voices Series Editors Bob Holman and Marjorie Tesser

ISBN: 978-0-9824012-4-8

Library of Congress Control Number 2010920857

Manufactured in the United States of America
or in the United Kingdom when distributed elsewhere

ver 10-02

Bowery Books are published in affiliation with

YBK Publishers, Inc.
39 Crosby Street,
New York, NY 10013

whose publisher, Otto Barz, is the inspiration for this series.
With thanks to Bill Adler.

My heartfelt thanks to family and friends who
have made/make this journey so very full;
to Dr. Ian Yudelman who has given me years
time and again in my battle with breast cancer;
to Mei Mei Hammer whose guiding
spirit has opened many doors;
and to Bob Holman and Marjorie Tesser
whose gentle patience/warm support
brought this book into fruition.

Fay Chiang, NYC   January 8, 2010

Bowery Books is the imprint of Bowery Arts and Science, a non-profit cultural organization. We are grateful for the assistance we receive from individual donors, foundations and government arts agencies. This publication is made possible with public funds from The New York State Council on the Arts, a state agency. We are grateful also for assistance from the Council for Literary Magazines and Presses.

for Xian

WIND

For Xian

Terror. I put a name to it, this feeling I have every night when I am unable to sleep: I walk around the apartment, wash floors, dishes, wonder how I will rearrange the shelves to hold more of my daughter's toys, books, drawings; turn on the TV, wait for the weather report, scan late night shows; make another cup of tea.

I look in on Xian, my seven year old daughter, fast asleep in her room. Her Christmas tree lights shine and I recall a conversation we had a few nights ago.

Xian, I'm going to get my energy back.
I know it's been hard the past few months.
–Mama, you'll lose energy by trying so
  hard to get it back. You'll waste energy.
Then how do I get my energy back?
–Oh, you just listen to me. Do what I tell
  you. I know how to keep my energy.
Okay, what's that?
–Mama, number one: Lie down;
  number two: Close your eyes;
  number three: Sleep.
Xian, you're so wise!
–And Mama, no talking!

I bargain. Let me get through this breast cancer. Let me live long enough to see my daughter grow up, until she doesn't need me. Then I realize she will always need me. Let me write a book, one good book, and let me have the health to go around this world, at least once.

Then I see her: a young woman riding a horse across the plains of Mongolia, braids flying against wind at ease with herself, her face shining with life and color, riding like a Native American princess from those storybooks of my childhood, living with nature taut, sparingly in the palm of the universe. I want to be those women: riding across the plains with the wind, with my daughter, her braids flying, our laughter ringing.

TABLE OF CONTENTS

Section I In the City Of Contradictions

Section II MIWA'S SONG

Section 3 MIDNIGHT BLUE SKY

Previous Publications and Credits

BOOKS PREVIOUSLY PUBLISHED

In The City of Contradictions edited and published by Virginia Scott, Sunbury Press, New York, 1979.

Miwa's Song, edited and published by Virginia Scott, Sunbury Press, New York, 1982

POEMS PREVIOUSLY PUBLISHED

"Tall Grasses Rippling in the Wind," *Ikon Magazine*, edited Susan Sherman, Ikon Press, NY, 1983

"Chinatown" excerpts published in *Voci dal Silenzio*, edited by Mario Maffi, I Canguri/Feltrinelli, Milan, 1996

"Flight," "Diving," *Tribes Magazine*, edited by Kathy Price, A Gathering of the Tribes, 2005

"Orchard Street," *Bowery Women: Poems*, edited by Bob Holman and Marjorie Tesser, Bowery Books, New York, 2006

"Wind," *The Mom Egg* IV, 2006, "Midnight Blue Sky," *The Mom Egg* V, 2007, "Seven Continents, Nine Lives (excerpt)", "In The Dim Afternoon Light," *The Mom Egg* VI, 2000. All issues edited by Alana Free and Marjorie Tesser.

"Monologue" is an excerpt from *Two Boots and A Ball Gown*, a two-act play.

"Chinatown" is an excerpt from the book-length poem, *Chinatown*.

"Flight" and "Days End" are poems from the book-length poem *In This Life*.

ILLUSTRATIONS

"Wind," pastel cover illustration, Copyright © Fay Chiang 2010

Credit and much thanks to Eve Arnold for use of her photograph, "CHINA. Inner Mongolia. Horse Training for the Militia," 1979, as a source for this illustration.

Section black and white linoleum and wood cut print illustrations, Copyright © Ding Kong 2010

    Section I   "Luxury Hotel for the Gentry, East Village, 2008"

    Section II "La Frontera: the 1,950 Mile-Long Open Wound"

    Section III "Resistance is Hope"

Calligraphy for the poem "Father" by Alex Chin, who also designed the original covers for the volumes *In The City of Contradictions* (1979) and *Miwa's Song* (1982). (Latter cover photograph by Harvey Wang).

Author photograph by Cathy Russell.

Cover design by Suzanne Altman.

In the City Of Contradictions

"Luxury Hotel for the Gentry, East Village, 2008" by Ding Kong

IN THE CITY OF CONTRADICTIONS

In the city of contradictions
    we are among the survivors
we, with our hands tool foundations
      in our songs, dreams and dances,
          our myths, legends, symbols,
             our systems of work

we see oceans in rain puddles
    grass blades grow from cement walks
and in the sky at night on Broadway
      the moon full, stars cry
          reminding us
             natural laws
                are to be remembered

we, who ride subways
    faces worn, dispirited with care
    we, who tend our homes, workplaces, families and friends

      wild at night in search

systematically trapped in identities,
      institutions, cornerstones of a society
         of prisoners screaming
                  in smoke
                  in drink
                  in disbelief
                      for release

the hope of South Africa
      thrives in
         this city

and we with our spirit, our love,
    we are among the survivors

spread the news

PARENTS

he,
    came to America
      aged 11 washing people's socks
        slept in class
    a paper son with false papers
      bought back in the village
        because America restricted   aliens.

I have a cameo photograph of him.
    New York Chinatown. 1939.
   out with the boys on Sunday
    (America only let the guys in)
hey! that dude was some snappy dresser.

during the war, they let him work
    the navy yards
      as an apprentice steel welder
        but when the soldiers came home

laundry customers called him,
                  Charlie.

she,
   came in 1950.
classified: refugee from China
 from the feudal backwoods of Kwantung
     her marriage arranged
        to New York rush hours.
speaking no English
    she worked in sewing factories
      till her back gave out.

they,
    raised a family
      in the backroom of a laundry,
        10' x 14', Queens, New York, 1950s.

there were:
> 1 folding table
> 6 folding chairs
> 1 convertible sofa
> 2 folding beds
> 1 baby crib
> 3 metal cabinets
> 1 black and white TV
> 1 sink
> 1 refrigerator
> 1 kitchen range with 2 burners
>> no heat. no hot water.

to earn money:
> a customer brought in a dirty garment
> received a ticket
> returned in 3 days.

in the meanwhile
> the garment was sorted
> marked in an inventory
> picked up by a commercial laundry
> washed
> returned the next day
> re-sorted
> starched
> hung to dry
> rolled to iron
> ironed
> packaged
> shelved with the other bundles.

in the '50s, one made
> a nickel   for each piece.

he: worked 6 days a week, 16 hours a day.
she: raised children, cooked, cleaned, sewed, worked in the laundry
      when she had time.
he: couldn't take it. he gambled with the boys.
she: told him to quit, or she would leave.
they: in the end (though it was not this simple) put down a mortgage on
      a little house.

the customers called him: Charlie
and her Mrs. Charlie.
he passed away from cancer
50 years old.
the relatives said he was a good man.

she misses her best friend,
continues the laundry
watching the children leave.
she hopes they graduate from college, marry,
have happy lives, grandchildren for her/him.

legacy:
the clarity of our own vision
what we choose to do with our own lives
will bear fruit to that
work/spirit.

CHINATOWN

I   mahjong and dice on the tables upstairs
        confusion of trucks and cars
           children, cats and dogs
              people falling off the mountain gold:

eddie died yesterday
      a street kid shot his fucking brains out
      and eddie's in heaven upstream east river
did you know
      mrs. tong jumped off her building
        looking for peace six stories above mott
and hey, old louey
      just passed away in his sleep
        the fool, sleeping with the gas pipes
                        on, again
did you hear about lee
      that he couldn't take his henpecking wife and
        screaming babies and rotten kids and waiter
        job and promises that couldn't be
        bought with pennies
        that he split before his head did?

II   december, 1956 from boston to new york
      I saw a sunrise on empty streets
        with old buildings and dark fire escapes
          people running
        to make a dime in factories, restaurants
          trying to beat time
          and make their american dream come true

      I ran
        in restaurants aged 10
          standing on milk cartons washing dishes
          folding papers for the china times
            stringing beads for the old lady
            and trying to be good
            and trying to be bad
          worrying about brothers and sisters being beat
            in the school yard
          being tough when I wanted to run

being smartass when I wanted to cry
trying to be big when I was really small

III   all the time
            walking on the poverty line
        all the time
            feeling the deprivation
                the wishing and the wanting:

american tv sold mickey mouse and donald ducks
    to little dick and janes and run spot run
        in the suburbias of white picket fences
            and automobiles
and american society sold cheap labor and self hatred
    to little chins and wongs and run dog run
        in the ghettos of railroad flats
            and dead end streets

I studied asians in america
    demonstrated against the war in indochina
        shouted *chilai! kaiho! amakibaka!*
    wrote newsletters, flyers,
        many times we leafleted and petitioned
            for community issues
    I struggled to learn to say and to believe:
        right on
            to people's struggle
        all power to the people

        there is a spirit and movement
            growing and pushing
        rearranging the order of things
            that nothing can hold back

TRANSACTIONS

chinatown. nyc. early 1950s. a crowded kitchen of an old tenement apartment, faucet leaking, clothing, towels drying, piles of newspapers, chairs, table with covered dishes of food and rice. the wife is seated and mending clothing at the table. it is almost midnight.

enter husband, puts down packages on table, takes off overcoat and hat, pours himself a drink, sits down at the table, places a newspaper at the wife's elbow, uncovers bowls, dishes of rice and begins to eat dinner.

wife: (continues mending and says in cantonese) what time is it?
(in english) what time is it?

husband: (casually talking through food) a little after 12. (silence. tension builds.) oh, I saw ah-lum on mott street. I was heading to the laundry association when he waved to me from hoy hong, had a cup of coffee with him, says his business is not doing well. I saw your mother's brother too, buying a newspaper.

wife: was it crowded at the credit union?

husband: nah. I got there around 10 am when they just opened. I put in 25 dollars (picking at food). ah lai and jen came back from san francisco, said they were trying to start a grocery store. a lot of them opening up out there. said he saw my cousin bing who might be coming out here this summer.

wife: (in cantonese) where are the groceries?

husband: so at the credit union, ah fat said what are you supposed to tell a white man what he doesn't know already, the bastards.

wife: (in english) where are the groceries?

husband: (points with chopsticks to paper bags) over there. I was telling ah lum that if the prices of the commercial laundries get any higher, we'll all be in trouble. he was saying we should all pick up a little dry cleaning to add a few dollars a week to our income.

wife: (puts down a few stalks of bok choy) is this all?

husband: the vegetables didn't look so good today.

wife: and I guess the fish didn't look fresh by the time you got there...

husband well....

wife: how much was it this time (irritably)

husband: (in chinese) 50 dollars. (in english) 50 dollars.

wife: (repeating dully) 50 dollars?

husband: I went up to see the *hingdai* at the family association and they were playing mahjong and this guy lays down some cards....(tension builds)

wife: (in chinese) do you think money grows on trees? (in english) do you think money grows on trees? how many times do you think we're going to get rich quick?! look at the 5,000 dollars we lost on the stocks and the other time, you and stupid hong buying some crazy land in arizona. why don't you work harder. look at ah lum, he's got a house now and what do you do? all the time reading, reading your books. can you feed the children on your books?! if you're so smart, why are we here? you've been here in america since you were 13, why are we still living in the laundry.

(while the wife is ranting, the husband continues eating dinner, pouring tea, trying to appear calm)

FOR PETER

I   walking to the end of the earth
              we jumped
              your mind burst
                   into a thousand stars
                       that shone
                          intensely
             ashes scattered in the winds

           trance-like you sat/on the bed
             in the hospital
                four walls
                    a shell

II   it is in this cold country
                the soul turns to ice—
                  reflections too clear
                     edges sharp—
                with trembling that threatens to
                            shatter

          it is in this realm
             lifefire
                burns like the starsun
                 refusing
                    to die

WALKING THE MOUNTAIN

the car stopped on the gravel driveway, we unloaded the pail and boiled chicken, steaming white rice, fruits and made our way under the arches leading to the burial grounds and monuments of those who came from sunwei, china; now resting in cypress hills, brooklyn.

we laid the brown paper down, my mother's instructions fighting with the wind as we set the chopsticks and bowls, cups of wine, baskets of fruits and a newspaper to read after the meal. my brother lit the pail and began lighting incense, candles and burning paper money to be carried by the smoke to the heavens.

and I was reminded three years past, how we had stood at the foot of the grave watching my father's casket being lowered, how my mother almost fell in after it.

how the following year, grandfather died two weeks prior to the anniversary of dad's death, how we wore the same clothes, again, how gruesomely and painfully the mourning was repeated.

how last year, my brother had a nervous breakdown and ranted in the house against ghosts from his mind and sang wild songs and did not sleep or eat and bled at the recurrences of his cancer, how we feared for his mind hemorrhaging, for our own safety in his walks during the night in the house with love/hate in his eyes and knives in his hands, how I almost broke down with him.

how during the last year we have made our transitions: my mother defining her identity and life in her own right; my sister's marriage and leaving; my other sister's life in her work and ceramic making; my own wrestling of the mind torn in confusion and grieving for a lost self:

> how early this spring I looked into a garden below wet with dew. birds raucous with hunger, thinking I should fall out and end the drone and pressure in my head. then a friend caught me and watched me for three days and two nights going clear out of my skull communing with dark fear, a fight with jumbled keys, jagged notes, images incoherent.

we stood at the "table" and made offerings while my mother spoke with him, reporting the current events: we paid off the real estate taxes that amounted to 4,000 dollars; the children are well; see your new son-in-law, aren't you glad one of them is married to such a nice person.

we packed up the bowls, teacups and she continued speaking to him there below the ground. we walked a little away, leaving the two of them, that perhaps they would commune in memories past, not buried, living with the passage of the seasons.

IN THE MIRROR THE FACE WAS NOT MINE

in the mirror the face was not mine, staring blankly, eyes gouged with shadows, hair uncombed, mouth limp, breathing shallow, eyes dull and lifeless.

> eyes   that were once shining and alert, hopeful, careless, open to vision, people
>
> other times shooting anger, mean, echoing ugly words that rang out in disbelief, in horror, in strong emotion   with conviction
>
> cat face secretive with child's games
>
> bursting in laughter
>
> soaring on wind and crazy energy like comets

this was a shell. a coward brined in self pity. I turned in disgust, rage   at myself.

A WOMAN SPEAKS

forgot to turn down the shade
   you always do
     left the iron on, too

well, I don't want much
   a change of clothes
     this old book of poetry
       we found on the curb
     my toothbrush will feel good
       an extra shopping bag
        in case I need
          more room
    these photo booth shots
      on our way to cape cod
        in the rain
    paper and pencil to keep track
      credit card/checkbook/cash
    good walking shoes
       and a flashlight for
         dark times

you keep the rest
   I don't want things
     or closed spaces I can't breathe in
   I need light, and air, and blue sky,
     people who are not afraid
       to feel fear, anger, hurt, pain, sorrow,
      hate, jealousies,

      laughter, ease, warmth, touch,
      humor, ecstasy, joy and love

   life and living
     taut with the knowledge of being alive
      and what that means

keep the accounts of the accounts
the matching silverware, matching chinaware,
the matching linens and tennis outfits,
        the collections of the collections,
                your bottles of liquor
            dust them, they're yours now

        explain to the children,
            best as you can.
        the fridge is on defrost,
            the roast will be done
                    by 6

        I've got to go

1 not take it, she flew on a high one night down five stories of
and bounced on the concrete street below. We used to climb
ther when she was doped up, because it was the only way she
all that hyped up energy out of her waif-like body. And she
was always asking me not to leave her alone like all the other people
who promised to come back. She hitched cross country, looking for
love and found it one time with a bunch of vagabonds messing around
with shit and snow. You know, it was not hard to lose track of time.

Little Leah with the sniveling, running nose. We climbed fences and
watched the moon in trances; dreamt there were fairies and elves doing
dances on Catherine Street and Madison at night in the summer by the
park. We could do anything we wanted to. Even now the junkies are out
on Rutgers, waltzing in three quarter time.

Do you know, do you know, do you know what it is like to be pulled, to
be pulled ten thousand places running out of energy fast? Do you know
what it means to be there in full and supportive when you are needed?
Do you know, do you know in ten thousand places going full cycle and
do you know I struggle to find space for rest and a place to place all
this?

And what it feels like to push others off their asses when they are
feeling low and down and doped out by the fact that we cannot get
anywhere. The sense of futility, giving up hope and the limitations,
gauntlets to be run? Do you know the nausea of being on the floor, half
conscious, being sucked by the grip of breaking down?

Do you know we've got to keep trying and trying and trying because it
is important to keep pushing in the morning to deal with the day, that
there are people and dreams to be built, that it is a struggle to know
this fucking society and ruling class have got it down to the nail poor
folks ain't worth anything, that we are peripheral and superfluous. Con-
sciously there are people hungry at night, children without food, medi-
cine, clothing, housing in the wealthiest country in the world.

We don't have a chance, if we don't take it.

SURVIVOR

they smell a survivor
   get down, ease on over
      lay back low
   get out of here

from pinnacles and top hats/monocles
   waving flags and marching bands
      sitting rooms/theater halls
         ivy covered study halls
   they—who need to retain/maintain
                              what they got

from country clubs and condominiums
      cadillacs on credit
      Caribbean weekends
            opening shows
      they—who desire pinnacles/waving flags
         deny place of origin
                           what they getting

from back alleys, street corners
      3 a.m.s of no eat/no heat/defeat
            television/barrooms/showhalls
      they—who are trying to survive with
                           what they never got

they all gonna tell you:
      you crazy if you question the way things are
      you mad if you think there is something terribly wrong
      you dangerous and got to be put away if you try
            to change the way things are

it's all right
      question
      think
      change

            baby, just be cool
               they burned witches in salem

IMAGES

image 1: Jesus Light My Fire

friday after the fundraiser event we were walking the three of us down second avenue to buy some ice cream on st. mark's place and this old woman in raggedy coat and kerchief tied round her face with grayish wisps of hair (it was a cool night, but spring enough to go walking) followed us pleading for us to sing to her, to play the guitar to her, to speak to her, we walked a little faster, she walked a little faster and said as we approached the bodega at the corner:

> I say, see the man in the corner sitting with his hands folded to his chest (indeed he was wearing a purple shirt and had a mustache and a terribly disinterested look on his face). well, that louse wouldn't give a starving grandmother or a starving nun, which I am, and I will let you know, I am an artist, but I do not want to go on with this, but he wouldn't give me a dollar's credit and you know what I'm gonna do, I'm gonna go up to his window and stick my nose at his face and give it to him, the bastard. (which she did, which I thought was terrific and told her so. We quickly developed a rapport, the other two had quickened their paces).

I'm an artist nun, dear. and you know that lesbian bar on bleecker. (I think so, murmuring politely. My friend who lives three doors away has mentioned it to me). Well, do you know that rock song, it was on the radio a few years ago...come on baby light my fire? do you know that I went into that bar and sang: come on jesus light my fire? which the both of us thought was hilarious: a starving nun on a dollar's credit singing jesus light my fire in a lesbian bar. we parted.

image 2: Let It Be Known

april 1970. antiwar scene, washington, d.c.

> bring the boys home. a naked man dances in the reflecting pool with a red, white and blue ribbon bow on his penis. a circus carnival atmosphere prevails. a contingent marches here and another there through the monuments and graves, the promenades of our country's vitals: socialists vs. trots, vs. commies vs......

new york city. 1970, 1971.
        uniformed policemen astride horses stomping impatiently in the
        winter wind cutting through the demonstration at the red cross
        lights while helicopters circled overhead beating moth-like wings;
        then the riot squad charged. fifth avenue, bryant park, wall
        street, columbia, duffy square, 125th street and lenox avenue.
        they came hurling down the street with the fucking bricks flying
        at us, and this one burly construction worker started beating the
        shit out of this kid next to me, and I started running and crying
        and the roar of the crowds and screams...they ran into trinity
        church beating wounded people.

1969 to 1972. campuses across the country. ethnic studies.
        we are asians in america with a heritage and culture, a history
        past, present and future to be proud of and we demand the fol-
        lowing non-negotiable demands, that ethnic studies is our right.

the question.
        I saw this photo of a woman crying over the plastic shrouded
        remains of her husband in life magazine. a vietnamese peasant
        woman shading her face with her hat and the saliva and tears
        falling off her face. though from photographs of black and white
        we do not smell, do not taste, do not touch, do not hear the pain
        and grief. in america we have become complacent and dull and
        numb and do not feel or hear or touch or see or smell our own
        pain and grief, alienation and hate. end the war. where is it?

image 3: Choices

so where does one go from here? down highway one in california there
is a road of radiant sunshine bursting with oceans and green growing
turf and a mellow way with waves, rock and seagulls at dawn.

other images recede: sounds and images of hurt, lost dreams and
people living on a thin line between realities which will never come true
to life, simply because of the economics of this capitalistic country.

last night there was a gentle wind on the roof as I watched the wind
blow the clouds across the moon face and I felt very tenderly the mor-
tality of it all. above there on the roof and tree tops, above the street

noise, people doing their business, in the houses and apartments with bright lights blinking in the distance, a constant stream of airplanes leaving for all parts of the globe and

there are nights I cannot sleep and rise agitated, to ponder in wearied brain fever the things that each of us must do and responsibility we have in making the changes necessary for social revolution. each time there is a personal struggle there is a narrowing of choices in cutting away those things superfluous, artificial.

in this lifetime, we should see the world and its people, travel directly to the continents and america, our own country, and taste the ways of people not from books or television perpetuating empty, mind mad t.v. syndicates and soap ads brillo-ing into middle america with madison avenue slickness.

destroy stereotypes we have been fed about one another: indians ain't tonto and neither were the blacks steppin' fetchit or the asians bred from charlie chan and the chicanos weren't half baked little people in god's oven. and all them blue-eyed devils are not one and the same. even now the hills of appalachia hide the poor white children of debtors from the days of colonial america. class is not easily erasable.

on the highway one never has to stop for long except to fill up on gas and take a leak once in awhile and stop for something to eat and drink; then it's on to the mardi gras in louisiana when it's festival time, or dig on oranges in florida or the deserts in the southwest or the frozen earth in fairbanks, alaska. something like that.

I will do this: scan skies with eyes thirsting for answers.

JOURNAL ENTRY
BASEMENT 199

getting the electricity hooked up in the loft has been one experience: it all started by calling Chino who told me to get Bimbo who hooked me up with Angelo who took days to reach and days to get up to the loft.

went down to 6th street the other night where Bimbo was working with Rabbit, Chino, Luis and Elsie mixing cement to put cinderblocks into the building windows Teatro was in the process of buying from the city, fire-proofing it from vandals. back and forth I walked from 6th street to the stoop on 3rd street where Angelo was waiting for the babysitter to come and watch his two kids. finally by 2:30 am, Bimbo came instead to 199 to test out the electrical lines by flashlight, promising to come back the next day with Charlie his electrician friend to design new electrical lines.

when we were in the loft, I said, Bimbo, it scares me, this space. I told him what other people were telling me, that the space was too big.

Bimbo said, it's all in the Dream. You've got to to keep the Dream honest and pure and if that was the focus, then it would work. that it was going to take sacrifices and a lot of hard work. if you weren't afraid of work, then you had nothing to fear and there will be people who will tell you that you are crazy and all kinds of ugly things for all kinds of reasons, but if you feel that it's the right time, then you put everything into the Dream, there's no holding back. he says: Fay, look here you can start some small industry to pay the rent or have parties. that's it, we'll come help you raise the rent money. what is 800 dollars?! many things will happen.

I asked him how he had decided to become a poet. he said he had gone to CCNY, got his M.A. working under a fellowship, with 11 years at the Transit Authority at night and was making 20,000, raising a family. but it was time to put all that aside and to work on his dream for Teatro. he had heard about Jorge Brandon, a sign painter, who kept a storefront on pike street and read poetry in the streets, this old man. they challenged each other to a duel of words and tried to out recite one another on east 6th street, while people threw things at them from the windows above telling them to shut up and they went on and on for hours until they both called it a draw.

Jorge started training Bimbo by sitting in a bathtub through two months of summer while Bimbo was working on his and Margie's apartment. talking about writing, about a vision of theater for the people, all through the summer he talked and Bimbo wrote. then, Jorge officially named Bimbo, a poet, and they got a storefront on 6th street. El Coco Que Habla. a prophet. a poet. El Teatro Ambulante.

Bimbo said he came to the decision to quit his job, the security. he sat down with his family and his older daughters said, yeah, daddy, we're behind you. so he says, you know, Fay, it comes to 14 cents an hour, but we have to do it. we have to give it a try. go for broke. and if we make mistakes, at least we would have tried and learned from it.

walking back to 6th street with Bimbo, carrying a pail full of tools for Chino and the work on the building, I told Bimbo I felt much better having talked with him. he said, you know the way "they" had it, we were never meant to meet and here we are!

on 6th street at 4 in the morning, people from Teatro Ambulante, Charas, 4th street "Eye" were frying salted fish pancakes on cinderblocks, warming hands, bodies from the flames, continuing the work.

I left walking down first avenue heading back to the loft, thinking and thinking about the Dream of Basement Workshop: an Asian American cultural center with music, dance, pictures, oral histories and stories to be told and written by little children, young people and older men and women my parents' age, working, learning and laughing with all kinds of people from many parts of the city, the country, the world in this part of the universe, this lifetime. too many people are too often broken-down and broken-hearted to have and to believe in dreams, afraid to take risks. if we do not have visions, then what is the use of all this.

we must feed the Dream.

FATHER

his long tapered fingers
  guide my young hand curved around
   a bamboo brush pen
    to form my name in chinese:

      family name: *chiang:* from northern china
        we came south on tamed wild horses
        and became farmers

      middle name: *wei*: shared by you
        and your sisters, meaning wisdom

      and your own *ping*: for peace
        or plains of green field

bits of characters:
  grass, heart, three dots of water, woods, home

  write again and again, your name,
      that you may never forget it

BREEZE

You come like a breeze   gentle
     like an ocean with
         undercurrents and deep wells
           pools swallowing gulps
         that become galloping
           hoof beats thundering/thrashing
             across brush and foliage
         growth on the forest floor
           catching ankles whose forces
         finally catapult toward sun
           then dark, a silence
         senses forced to attention, yes,
           of all
             that is possible.

BITTER STRENGTH

bitter is
        unshed tears
        hollow eyes burnt
        is tight jaws locked behind screams
                of rage and anger
           clenched fists
bitter is
        nightmares in warped time
        memories walking solitary paths, the place of birth forgotten
        the crashing of spirit on rock
bitter is
        battered souls flying/circling disembodied
        a lifetime: once, not repeated
strength is
        the will to survive
          from fires of lives refusing to die
        voices wrenched from guts
        minds, spirits laced with lava
        all willed, hammered to
                endure

bitter strength feels the sun
        on foreheads and backs bent over fields
        on hands shaped by labor
          feet planted in earth
bitter strength knows its ties
        to the people: the children, the mothers,
        the fathers, the sisters and brothers,
        cousins, aunts and uncles, the lovers and friends;
        knows the support, the love, that we give and take,
        the need to know: place of birth, context, purpose
        and continuity
bitter strength takes comfort and warmth
        in the hearts, the songs and stories,
        the meals eaten together,
        the small events, secrets, repeated

bitter strength knows
    it was:
        Black enslaved in cotton
        Chicano, Filipino migrant workers
        Native American destroyed by genocide
        Appalachian poor white
        Asian American in concentration camps
        fueling the growth of skyscrapers and automobiles, wall street
        and wars overseas, empires and stockades of wealth and power;
        engendering seeds of bitterness:
        in the cotton fields of India
        the ghettos of Puerto Rico and South America
        the genocide of blacks in Africa, the Caribbean
        the coal miners of Wales
        and farmers in Asia
        in the people the need to know
        place of birth, context, purpose and continuity

planting the seeds of
            revolution
bitter strength is not a thing of the past

bitter strength is our
        bloodline

HOME

three weeks in maine woods; sensibilities cleansed, thoughtfu
nature's own rhythm, unrushed, eternal. country roads at nigh
lit, star shone protected by towering pines, comfort of lake wat
against earth banks and wind floating a symphony of night soun
insects, soft cooing of birds. baking grass, strawberries and wild
ers, crackling of weight upon earth textures, the wooded forest, sandy
beach, mud oozing by the bank. clouds shadow-play the lake surface.

entering the city through harlem on the greyhound, the city streets swel-
ter with people on stoops, children playing jump-rope, small business
doorways crowded with neighbors passing the day with small talk, a
bottle of beer, german shepherds run into fire hydrants spraying cool-
ness and rainbows, cars, buses honk and pedestrians cross red lights
with cool indifference. abandoned buildings gape at the windows, but
the city is vibrant with life. the bus driver gives the passengers a tour
of the city, its sites, and tells anecdotes of people who have changed
the streets they live on with beauty: murals by children, flower boxes
and the planting of trees in barrels, the cleaning of streets, community
people, churches rehabilitating buildings, tells us how people enjoy cen-
tral park and all the things one can do there throughout the year, that
the newspapers and the rest of the country don't know what it is talking
about when they put this city down.

walking down the strip on 42nd nodding to other travelers with back
packs, taking in the neon, the crowds of hustlers and office workers,
pass the stone lions at the library, I enter the subway.

mama is ironing shirts this afternoon. I put down my bags, canvases.
the rice is on the stove and there's some food on the table, tea in the
pot, she says simply continuing her work.

in the back room next to the rice barrel and the stove papa found on
the street and fixed, I gaze at the brown packages of laundry, some old
enough to have papa's writing on it, others with mine on the laundry
tickets and now with mama's; the wooden shelving with the dark green
trim papa built one sunday when the store was closed, the linoleum he

.id the uncles put down on another. next to the stove, the sink with cold water we mixed starch for collars and shirt cuffs, washed down the dinner greens, water for tea.

a customer comes in and talks to mama about the weather, the supermarket bargains across the street and bobo, our dog, sleeping in the sun. mama says, those are my daughter's. she just came home. I hear the voices, the moments and remember the daily gatherings at meal time, rituals, the leaving, coming back in our family.

I am full, eating steamed rice.

FOUND LETTER POEM

dear richard:
I like working on the house.
mostly been scraping off old paint.
the morning's discovery:
between one of the layers
(the house is about
50 years old)
of paint, I found some
children's crayon marks
something like two and a half feet
off the ground.

I was moved, speechless.

urban archaeology:
who was this child?
during which ring of paint
was it marked?
ought I scrape off
a sample
and go through some
mumbo jumbo test
over the kitchen stove?
what has become of this child?

time becomes this
very intangible thing.

love, fay
may 12, 1976

A POEM FOR RICHARD

I the spirit moves you
    onto new landscapes,
      needs developing for years
       must be fed

   life fire burns
    coaxed with bits of
      dried grass
     twigs
       branches charred
        into flames
       lighting us through dark passages
         of terror

   throats murmuring
    in the autumn evening
     we dare laugh at stars,
      tree shadows, clouds
       still with wonder

II I will stay in the city
    shake hands on the lower east side with
     gypsies, magicians, artists, musicians,
     writers, organizers, children, people
      waltzing with prophets
        in the changing season
    learn new tongues
    from those who survive
     with tenacity, sheer will
      rebuilding communities
       from streets smoking
        like Hiroshima
        like Soweto
        like Watts
         on Avenue D
      from people with smudges
       where eyes should be
       toothy smiles communing with
        spirits we cannot see

there are those fighting
        like prizefighters
            against the city, the state,
                the country of those who have power
                    against those who do not
                        shadowboxing
                            becoming resilient
                                empowered by vision, little else,
                    with all logical odds against them,
                        they enter and fight

        I join them
            whose same anger
                deep hungers
                    run through my veins
                        ready to burst

III   I will learn to build a purposeful life
            to choose human honesty
            to weld my will into steel
                my mind like a knife, sharp;
                when thrust, to draw blood,
                    to get up when struck,
                        bent on winning

    I stay in the city
        six stories above ground
            facing south, brick walls
                off the bowery,
            make curtains for this
                tenement flat, aged with paint

    I hope
        there will be hot water, heat in winter
        2 chairs, table, bed,
        books, paint, brushes,
        canvas, a teakettle,
            gates on every window
                locking out burglars
                locking me in

there are wrinkles on my forehead,
 now the face in the mirror changed
  a little sad
    eyes wet and brown like
     a dog's or farm cow's
    hands thickened from holding others
     hammers and loads
        mouth set in a straight line

between the writing and painting
 I scoop ice cream in Soho
  paste up mechanicals
   work seasonal sales
   at minimum wage
     subsistence
    Medicaid, food stamp forms
     waiting
    gambling with pennies, nickels,
     time and my life

IV   In midwinter
   when streets are blanketed with snow
    and most harsh,
      will you write
       to tell me the news
      is the wind scented with ocean breezes and green
       in the Bay area?
      are people just as crazy?
     will you drink coffee or tea
        depending on your budget
      and if you still like
        slow Sundays, dinner at 3
     of course, the work,
       how is the writing and music,
         your voice,
        how is all of that

I will unfold your letters
  over a cup of tea
    thoughts wandering back to

poetry on Catherine Street fire escapes
        Chinatown families weaving home
                factories still
        picking up roast pork
            a few oranges, a pound of bokchoy,
        children after school
                old ladies on milk cartons by P.S. 1 park
                    disassembling for dinner

on 8th street
        snowball fights under
            the arch in Washington Square Park,
        Maine woods, Montauk dunes,
            poetry readings in Boston, Princeton,
        upstate rides back home
                huddled against
            sleeping bags and guitars
                empty coffee cups, early morning

writing sessions sharing our
        secret selves
            laughing, always the laughter,
            tea at Mamie's or MeiLai Wah   for years
        where in lowered tones
            I saw dishes flying in your childhood
                evacuation, FBI at home doors
        and you heard my family's
            madnesses and deaths rage

how in five years
        we built with frustration
            driven by our own need
                to validate ourselves, families,
            our friends, our Asian American-ness,
            our writing, beginning as tentative as we were
                becoming bold, loud,
                    the seeds of an Asian American literature
                    on the east coast

            we   did   that

33

with other writers, dancers, musicians, artists
legitimizing our anger and feelings
and know that we have done
good

V   in the quietest moments
I am not brave
remember how you
in your way
sustained me
with words, questions,
gestures, love

many times a better knowledge
of me/my needs
a thread to a wildly
spiraling kite,
earthbound, steady, loyal
"You can't do everything at once"
I've slowly learned that,
hold onto it
in the worst times

let's see what will happen
you facing the pacific
I with angels and dark spirits on the lower east side
with nothing to lose, all to gain

our friendship ripening

Miwa's Song

"La Frontera: the 1,950 Mile-Long Open Wound" by Ding Kong

MIWA'S SONG

We lie on the bed after reading a story about Barbar
and Celeste in the Animal Kingdom. A soft light
shines from her Winnie the Pooh lamp.

> Are you 5 years old yet? I remember when you were 2.
> -Well, I'm going to be 6 soon. In six months I think.
> Are you thinking of presents yet?
> -Yes.
> Oh. Maybe you shouldn't tell me, then you won't
> be surprised.
> -I'll be having such a good time with life, I'll
> forget and then it will be a surprise.
> Oh.

We lie still. I am the one falling asleep smelling
the wool blanket and scent of a child's smooth skin
and soft hair.

> She says abruptly, Do you know what a globe is?
> -What? Where did you hear about a globe? Do you
> mean a glove?
> No. A globe is round and has a picture of the
> whole world on it.
> -Oh. (I see her years from now, a world traveler.)
> I would really like a globe. One with a pencil
> sharpener on it, okay?

IN CHIAPAS

door ajar
   balcony lights sift through dusk
      form shadows
         on these pages
from the rooms of the hotelkeeper
   I smell supper
      imagine silverware, plates
        being set on a table
    I hold *un vaso de café*
       writing letters home

smoke hanging in cold air
   chimes ring across valley
      mist and clouds against cerulean sky
   play with sunlight
      her shadows on green mountainsides
   then rain bursts from thunder
      chill blankets night

in the market
   Chiapas men load wares
      fruit, sandals, bags of grain
   women fold children, piglets,
      chickens into shawls
  leading horses
     they head home
       towards crowing roosters
        burning fires

down cobble-stoned roads
   I pass shopkeepers locking doors
     drawing shades
       arroz y pollo   *sopa de ajo*
    fill my nostrils

in the *zocalo*
    the corn woman husks   ears of maize
      worn, strong fingers
        toss them into small buckets
        of boiling water
      I buy one of these   *cinco pesos*
       a handful of peanuts
         stride on

I watch the old man
   on the stone steps
     of san cristobal de las casas
  pour water from altar vases
    down a hillside
    then drying his hands
      on the legs of his pants
 he ascends slowly to the belfry
    pulls on a sisal rope
     bells signaling
       the evening hour

THE BUS FROM MERIDA TO PUERTA JUAREZ

vultures spring from a rabbit
        lying in the road
        bus swerves
        we go on

a little girl in magenta dress
        barefoot along wheel tracks

at a crossing a mayan mother
        covers her baby
        her shawl shielding its face
        from raindrops

children in yards of
        thatched-roof homes
        lost in games
        smiles from wind souls singing
        whispering magic in their ears

father and son carry firewood
        emerge from the forest
        bands of leather across foreheads
        neck taut, backs bent
        arms curved
        hugging the weight to waists
        walk dusty roads under scorching sun
          like their mothers and fathers
            before them

men build structures in a clearing
        sweat falling from brows
        they stand up, stretch, bend
          again with tool in hand
            sand shifts to water
              becomes cement

women's presence here
        four towels, a child's dress

a pair of men's pants
    waving from a wash line
she stops sweeping her doorway
    broom in hand
      pausing to chat
        with her friend returning
        from the market

pass little towns
    where children and little dogs
    run in circles
    the driver slows his bus
    clouds suspended from skies
      like fluffy boats
    yucca plants/spiky hands
      reaching for rain

over there
    a cornfield for family, goat,
    horse tethered grazing
    in front of the house

church bells, usually three
    aged with the flatlands
    rusty from centuries
      of mid-afternoon showers at two
    generations of priests
      mass and congregations

I sit behind the driver
    playing his collection of tapes
      mexican singers wailing
        wind, mist, cries
        from chiapas
      segue into disco and
        beatles abbey road
        magical mystery tour
      on the road from merida
        to puerta juarez

at a place where sky
    joins earth

DOLPHINS IN THE BAY

schools of glimmering fish nibbling ankles and
shins, I swim away from them in the Caribbean
and think of dolphins I saw in the bay hurtling
their bodies towards sun, leaping, their spines
twisting into graceful arcs.

I am one of them, back arched, face tightening
under the noonday sun, water gliding by thighs.
I trickle water with finger tips and gulp the smell
of smoky fish from open fires by the shore.
pure white. there is silence, sky, clouds in round,
soft formations glimmering with rainbows.

I feel cool and think of mermaids riding the
backs of dolphins and whales, water streaming,
pushing, I glide.

AFTERNOON SHOWER

I   Jungle reaching beach
         sand dissolving in ocean
         water breathing sky.
         Put a Mayan temple in this.
         A *cenote* across the way is
            filled with rain, root,
            human sacrifices
                  hundreds of years old.

      At this site
         a family sells Coke and Pepsi.
         Children play make believe store
                using palm leaves for pesos.

      It rains at two.
         Sheltered by a shack
         I watch torrents of
            white grey sheets
            drumming stone, grass, tree,
            earth drinking;
         wonder if this was not what
            my parents did as children
            walking roads in farmland
                among ruins and Buddhist shrines,
                fields of corn and rice.

II   I was told towns and villages were
            just clusters
            of buildings, small stores.
            Children watching travelers
            on vehicles passing through,
            their eyes wide with curiosity
            at strangers speaking
                foreign tongues and using
                cameras capturing images
                they will never see.

When she was ten
            soldiers came into the village
                with boots, guns, bullets.
            My mother and the village children
                ran after them
                looking into their faces
                wanting to know what
                    they were thinking.
            These were Japanese soldiers
                invading China in the '30s,
                passing through on
                    their way to
                        battles of greater importance.
                    In the backwoods of Canton,
                        they smiled at children
                        and gave them coins, chocolates.

III   In Singapore
      monkeys and parrots lived in trees.
      At times a tiger would
        invade the yards
        running off with chickens,
        even eating a man.
Once, there were snakes
      that swallowed children—whole—
      if they weren't careful.

Having caught such a snake
      the village people cut it open
      found the bones
      of a little boy
      who had not come home
        for supper
        a year or so ago.

This is Singapore where
      my uncles and aunts as children
        could not leave the yard
        when their parents went to work
        their father, a day laborer
        their mother a domestic.
     They spent their days
       scratching lazy pigs
       cooling their backs
       with buckets of water
       fattening them to sell
         under Harvest moons.

IV   A Mayan woman washes dishes
        in the sink the size of a pot
           behind the counter
               of Café Caribe in Merida.
She wears a kerchief
        round her head;
           her hands scrub dishes and glasses.
               The waitress walks by her
               indifferently.
In front, patrons and tourists
        from South America and Europe wait,
           North Americans eat breakfasts,
           some read books alone,
           others write postcards,
           couples plan and
           sleepy children throw tantrums—
all making stacks of dirty dishes
        needing the hands
           of a Mayan woman.

On the outskirts of town
        a man climbs the steps
           from a yard into his house,
           takes off straw hat, work shoes
           and then, stretching
               looks skyward
               to see birds flying
                  against sunsets raw.
A hand shades his eyes,
        rubs fatigue away
           and taking a slow, deep breath
               he sits down to eat.

V   My aunt is a dishwasher
     in Singapore,
       the only one
         who did not come to America.
    She and her husband have
      seven children I have never seen,
     in a thatched tin-covered shack
      with chickens and pigs.
We have a photograph:
    they are smiling
      in their best dress
      In a studio with a backdrop
        of flowers and clouds
    sitting in finely carved chairs
      their lives frozen among palms
       for a brief moment.
    The one leaning against
      her father's knee
      looks like my youngest sister,
      especially the eyes and
      the smiling little mouth.

VI   Family-run in the '50s in Queens,
          my father, his cousin and a best friend
              operate a shirt-pressing factory
                  from two rented shops
                  and a basement.
      Having left China
              after the war and revolution,
          they lived with their young families
              in rooms upstairs
              sharing kitchen, living room,
                  bathroom.
      Below the shop employed
          those who could operate
              sewing machines for tailoring,
                  pressing machines for steaming shirts.
          For a few pennies extra,
              workers hand-pressed collars
              and cuffs standing
                  at ironing boards
                  10 hours a day
                  in 100 degree heat,
          while others folded garments
                  counted inventory
                  packed shirts in boxes
                  loaded them onto trucks
                  delivered them back
                      to local laundry stores
                      which were scattered
                      in the middle class communities
                          of those who sent out
                              their laundry.

VII   My sisters, brother and I
                    played in front of our laundry
                walked around our block
                        in Queens by LaGuardia airport
                        stealing flowers
                        from neighbors' gardens
                        for our mother
                                working in the laundry
                                with our father.
                Sometimes before sunset
                        we visited neighbors
                        from the old village
                        in China now living in
                        East Elmhurst.
                        One old man kept a rooster
                                in his yard
                                we chased in circles
                                        among the bokchoy
                                        summer squash
                                        and laughter of adults as
                                        dusk turned into twilight.

        When laundry customers spoke to us
                        we smiled, saying little.
                        Perhaps we looked solemn
                        with our eyes wide open,
                        standing together
                        in a cluster giggling.
                We were taught to be polite
                        to strangers whose laundry
                        our parents cleaned
                                so we may eat.

VIII   I cannot remember
         the shirt-pressing factory
         only my mother telling us
            how before mealtimes
            having cleaned the apartment,
            fed, changed, bathed and
            set the baby to nap,
         she went downstairs,
            washed vegetables,
            cut meat and prepared
            the noonday meal
               for 30 people working
               in the shirt-press factory.
            It was a custom from the village
            sharing the noonday meal,
            breaking from the 10 hour day.

She told us:
    There will always be the work
        to be done, still
           we must stop and eat,
               rest a little and talk.
        Sipping tea and eating
           oranges whose tang
           would scent the air
           their conversation centered
           on family, the world,
             price of things,
             weather and gossip.

IX   I have never seen the old country;
           the family home with apartments
           built around a courtyard tiled,
           the large central kitchen
           where all the women prepared meals
           with the help of servants;
       where as a young bride, my mother,
               began by boiling water
                for the iron rice pot
                       over an open fire;
       everyone eating together
               dogs begging for scraps,
               children running around
       all this behind a wall with a door
               opening to a street
               like ones I have seen
                       in Mexico.

       I am unfamiliar with
               parrots and monkeys in jungles
               chickens and pigs that need tending
               the heat when I am walking
                       a dusty road at noon.
       I think I will not find
               the right street or word.
                   I stare with open eyes,
                           walk quietly,
                           rearrange sensibilities.

X   Instead I find a language
         without words.
            It has something to do with
                gestures, hands,
                movements on a face,
          the light and humor from the eyes,
          posture and stance,
          arching of the neck,
          a toe sliding or
          gripping earth and of
          sounds coming from within:
                gurgling, laughter,
                moans like storms,
                wind through trees,
                and moods like lightening
                   before thunder.

         Signs of faith, talismans
         and rituals repeated by those
            who inhabit the earth
            repeated in different times,
                different places.

The afternoon shower stops.
         Figures move away from shelter, trees,
            doorways animating the road.

            Sun plays its final rays fleeting,
              washing clouds in rainbows,
             a gray smudge there
                disappearing on the horizon.

VOICES THAT HAVE FILLED MY DAY

dreaming you say thank you
I ask thank you for what?

someone yells Hector!
hey Julio! Hector! Julio!
no one is home

a breeze faint slides
pass curtains
Hells Angels gun bikes
down third towards the river
a window opens
conversation drifts upstairs
I can't hear what
they are saying

this sultry city night
recalls voices
that have filled my day

Mercedes is home from Toronto
you know about family
when you're away from them
you miss them
when you're with them
you want to get away
if ever understood
it's the stuff
to all great stories

at the office
Teddy and I work through
mailing lists
picking and sorting
names like seeds and burrs
carding from fiber
spinning thread to weave
a new season

in a magazine, a woman potter says
    I work for a life
       not of money and success
   but a life
       of human freedom and dignity

I meet Tomomi
    who Jean met in a hallway
     at the Instituto in San Miguel de Allende
       students in the university
       Jean digging clay
           from the Mexican earth
           hauling it to work
             with her hands
           spinning the wheel
               with her legs
           back bent, hands raising
               deftly wet, clean forms
              shaping a life
         Tomomi traveling and living
           in villages and homes
           of native artisans, weavers
           learning the art of
             backstrap weaving
           gathering, drying, grinding
             the humble cochineal bug
             brewing and testing
             its dyes over a boiling pot
             open fire
             steam rising like mist
             at morning over Mount Fuji
     their roads cross
           for a moment
           then hold

   we have coffee at Kate's
        who has been to Calcutta
        seeing poverty unbearable
           except those within it
           whose belief in the afterlife

            negates the presence
            of cholera streaming
            from infested English barracks
                on the hill, by the mouth
                on the stream
                feeding the city's thirst
            outraged, Kate storms
                to the Health Department
                he says why bother
                saving them from cholera
                if they will then die
                from malnutrition
                here in India
                it all evens out

Peter gets better in the hospital
            memories fading of a past
            once catching his footsteps
            and taking away the sound
      over the telephone
            he asks if I could bring
            some change, magazines, fruits
            I bring them tomorrow and
            we make plans to take a walk

we sit in a coffee shop in Chinatown
      MeiMei says I've begun to collect
            bones for you and
            I will lend you the
            beautiful horse skull
            someone has given me
            parched by sun on desert floor
            by brush, by cacti
            my house is adobe
                with a tin roof
                a wood-eating stove
                fed by the woodpile
                away from the water pump
      Teddy talks about light
            shafts of available light

                    in a four-foot square
                    in a darkened space
                    of a dance she travels in
                         with sounds
                                of chopping wood
                                water dripping from a faucet
                                her own breathing
                                the turning of a page
          We talk about movements
               in the universe
               and light, natural light
               the scale of all these things
               around us wonderingly

          in this darkened kitchen
               I recall dreams from a decade ago
                    dreams like stars
                    some fixed in constellations
                    others bursting like comets
                              fiery, sudden, gone

          down the hallway
          someone unlocks a door
          they've come home

          I thank you for the sunrise

JOURNAL ENTRY

the night dad died in the hospital, he was so weak, he couldn't move or pick up his hands. I held his hand and squeezed his fingers wondering if he felt the touch. watching him try to say something, his jaw locked tight. his mouth slightly open, making a sound from his throat: pushing, forcing, working all the muscles for the strength to utter sounds and trying to focus his oscillating eyes as they were losing control over nerves that would not work for him.

there wasn't anything I could do to help him as demons fought to pull him away from us in the room. we stood around the bed.

then he was crying, tears rolling down the inner corners of his eyes, breathing with much difficulty. I wiped the tears, patting the crown of his head in the way he used to comfort us when we were little and sick.

it's okay, dad, go to sleep. when you wake up, you'll be okay. he fell into a deep sleep.

I miss him. no answers to many questions. learning to be more open, to be able to express feelings to others without feeling ashamed or embarrassed, to be less afraid. wishing I could have shared, explained to him certain of my life choices.

AUTUMN DUSK

Autumn dusk seven years ago
  in a hospital room
  he lay dying of cancer
    in his last days.
  She came daily after classes
    with books and sketch pads
    had coffee with him
    smoothing out pillows
    small talk about weather
      never the pain or sorrow.
 On one of these late afternoons
   he sat up straight in bed
   recited his life events
   looking into air
   catching fragments
    wove his story
    sighed, lay down
    till shadows grew long.
  She listened in silence
    never having heard this
    remained still and taut
    as street lamps
      flickered on.

Here are words they may have spoken
  if they had known how to then

The Daughter speaks:

    Father, can I say I love you,
    that I'm proud to be your daughter
    I know we don't say
    these things in our family
    and we don't realize
    how quickly time goes by
    taking many things
    for granted

I couldn't say it then
in the hospital room
when you told me your life story
in less than ten minutes

Father, your life
was greater than that
somehow you came to this country
married, settled
I don't know how you did it
I'm too scared to try
you raised a family
with a laundry business
working without complaining
six days a week

I look at the photographs
you took with the Brownie camera
the family growing

When we kids were in our teens
we didn't want to go
with you and ma on Sundays
to parks and museums
because we were trying
to grow up, away
I hadn't thought about
a father missing
his children on Sundays

I feel sad sometimes
when I see autumn light
when I see children
with their fathers
that I can't tell you
all that's happened to me

Looking back
I see you were proud
of me in your way:

the morning I left
for Washington, DC
for my first NEA meeting
it was snowing
I was scared
you said you wanted to go
to the airport
for the ride—
at six o'clock in the morning!
We had coffee
my flight was called
you gave me the morning paper
pecked me on the cheek
saying good luck!

I found in your papers
a story from junior high school
I wrote
in your long flowing script
now it's the only copy
I have of it

We always had schemes
about real estate
how we would mortgage the house,
buy others, renovate to sell
buy one with a garden
for Ma filled with flowers
We would do this
with our hands

I want to tell you
how scared I was
when you died
Ma was hysterical,
frightened, pacing the house,
cleaning and re-cleaning
There was the laundry
to be run;
I didn't know how to do it

Father, I learned to
iron and starch
to package and wrap,
work 12 to 14 hour days
to help the family;
slowly Ma healed

Then when I thought
it was getting better
and I could carry on
with my life
Peter got sick;
it was hospitals
and emergency rooms again
On a bed he sat up
with blood pouring
from his mouth, his nose
onto his chest, on white sheets,
onto the nurses, doctors,
Ma and me
Peter saying he was all right;
Ma saying Peter was all right,
when it wasn't all right

I didn't feel anything
for the next two years

I was scared
but I thought of you
working in America at 10
you must have been scared
somehow you did it

I would too
I had two hands
and I thought I would try
very hard to build a life
I wanted you to be proud
of me, made believe
you were still here

You became Papa-in-the-Sky
when things went wrong
I would have conversations
with you in my head
and things would clear up

I was going to build a life
my writing to share
this pain, the ache
yes, joy in memories
and the hope that someday
I would understand all of this
I think I've begun to
Papa-in-the Sky

The Father speaks:

That afternoon in the hospital
   the autumn light pouring in
   you sitting
   at the foot of my bed
   with your school books
   and drawing pads
   dozing till the room
   was gray in dusk
   my eyes closed
   I thought of other autumns
   September, the month
   I was born in China
   seems so long ago.

   Father took me walking
   with him in the mountains
   looking for his burial plot
   to rest his bones, he said.
   He was 65 when I was born
   still a strong man
   he was rich now
   having worked the gambling houses
   in Victoria's Chinatown

and salmon canneries,
he could afford to prepare
for his old age.
Mother said he was foolish
taking me with him
since I hobbled
on my bad leg.

It was a bone disease
that kept me from running
with the other children.
I was different, dreamy,
reading books Father collected.

Abruptly I was told
to go to America
to support the family
Father, after you died
Mother sent me to work
with older brother in a laundry.
I couldn't study
the new language
washing socks at 6 am
till it was time for school
where I would fall asleep
then back to work
until midnight ironing, washing.
I fell asleep on
the ironing board
it was my bed.

This was being a man
like you, Father,
and my older brothers
we left the village
to work overseas
and send money home;
hoping to return home
ourselves one day.

I stopped school in 8th grade
and continued working
in that laundry in Staten Island
Sundays I would meet the hingdai
from the village in Chinatown
to eat, gamble a little.

Some of the young men
went to whorehouses, but
I spent them with Paul
over at Old Man Chiang's place.
He had three daughters
and we'd go on picnics
at Coney Island, Central Park.
Chiang's daughters were
so Americanized
he had to offer
a thousand dollar dowry
for each daughter
and this was in the 1930s!

During the war
I couldn't join up
it was the old foot that
couldn't run fast enough
so I worked the shipyards
over in Brooklyn
welding on scaffolds
sides of ships
making the most money
I'd ever seen.

I met Leo and Ruth at church
an older couple
who showed me a photograph
of a niece of theirs
in China, the next village over.
She was so sweet and innocent
looking, I thought
I would go back home to see

if she was willing to marry.
Paul said he wasn't ready
to settle down and
wanted a city girl
but I wanted someone like myself
from the country at the
foothills of the mountains.

Our marriage was arranged
traditionally,
which wasn't easy for your Ma;
then we lost two babies
a boy, then a girl
one less than a month and
the other stillborn.
Her grandmother said
because your Ma was raised alone
without her family
she was especially shy,
frail in health and
if I were patient, gentle
she would strengthen with time.

We were in Hong Kong
at the time of the revolution.
Her Uncle Leo sent for us
to come to New York;
leaving behind
family, friends,
our wedding gifts and all our belongings.

With money from friends
we started a shirt pressing factory
but Paul, Bing and I
weren't businessmen—
we were young, didn't know enough;
we lost money and
closed the place down.

I had you to support
and your ma was pregnant with Jeannie
Paul and Bing wanted me
to go with them to California and
go into the grocery business.
Your ma wanted to stay
here in New York
close to Uncle Andy and Aunt Ruth.
I was torn because
I'd been in New York
with Paul and Bing
since we were kids,
but I couldn't leave your ma.

The first few years
in Queens passed by so quickly
I tried to make
the business work.
Many times it got too much.
I know I was wrong
when I went to Chinatown
and gambled all
the food money away
and got your ma angry
and all of us hungry.

I was young
almost as young as you now
with a wife
and four kids living
in back of the laundry
and the debt still to pay off
from the shirt-pressing factory.
I know your ma, you, we all
deserved better than that.
I was doing all that I knew
the best I could.

I think you knew
you were always quiet

your eyes bigger than your mouth
watching, taking care of
the kids, when your ma was tired.

In this country
it's not like China—
I would raise
and teach you
to be a son.

When you were 5
I remember holding your hand
teaching you calligraphy
black ink on white paper
after kindergarten
you sat for hours
writing characters
feeding your baby brother
in between.

I was proud of you
winning those writing contests
writing in English
something I never
had the time to learn

The chance to learn
I wanted you to have
the chance to learn,
the time I didn't have
I didn't want you to worry
about the things I had to
when I came here at 11
working all the time
like a man
not having free money
to spend or new clothes
to wear.

I didn't want you to work
in the laundry too much
only enough for you to know
you must help your family
in a little way.
Your grandfather and I
were proud of you
going to Washington
somehow the times had changed
people were angry
you didn't have to be afraid
like my generation.

I am not dozing
just thinking with my eyes closed.
Sneaky, as my mother
would say in China

This is my last September

I am scared of dying

I will not see you grow up

I have known of this dying
    this cancer eating me up
        the nightmares
            and hospitals

this pain in my stomach

these tubes and needles

these drugs that separate
    my body from my mind

the way my body has shriveled
    with this cancer

that once held you

that picked you up when you fell

that built a laundry from scratch
   that used tools, my hands
   which taught you to use tools
      to build

that carried weights and loads

that is limp

that is decaying

that is dying

I had to tell you
my life in those sentences
I had to hear it out loud
to let you know my fear
the pain that has been searing me
for two years
and the sorrow and pain
as I saw you
at the foot of my bed
in a chair with your
books and your drawings
in this light
in this autumn light
this September.

SNOW

Snow falls in a hush under night lights, lampposts doing waltzes. I feel hopeful, though logic says to worry. We run out of money with budget cuts in the arts, in unemployment, food stamps, Medicaid, housing. We've got two hands apiece, we'll figure something out.

It snows now. Tops of buildings covered white and figures walking slowly past drifts on streets below. Spirits smoke-like float on each snowflake searching for kin.

Put away the papers, stack the work for tomorrow, turn the calendar page. Each time the ritual prepares for a new beginning. I walk slowly down seven flights of darkened wooden stairs, past other lofts filled with oiled machinery for small industries. The front door opens and my coat is caught by chill seeping through a hole in the right pocket. Shuddering I walk towards Spring Street, past the iron security gates of the carpenter, the Chinese family coffee shop, the rice and beans restaurant, the corner smoke shop. People have gone home. They must be eating supper, maybe watching t.v. or preparing a sandwich to take to work, school. Or maybe sick in bed with this flu.

Down Spring Street there are silent side streets, loading bays scattered in snow, by workers hurrying home at 5 pm. Windows reflect snow, lamplight. They are eyes. I look past instead staring skyward and search the darkness for the source of this snow. There are many snowflakes and they swirl in patterns like messengers, their secrets entwined in one another, my figure swept up by their dances, in motion.

I am excited: a warm glow in my chest expanding, breathing. There is a song about living, about being. I hear it when I walk through snow under lamplight in city streets.

Midnight Blue Sky

"Resistance is Hope" by Ding Kong

MONOLOGUE

I knew I had to leave home. I was exhausted after a year of student activism: anti-war organizing, struggling with other students to institutionalize Black and Puerto Rican, Asian American, women's, and gay studies. Fitting art and painting classes in between.

I facilitated a class on Asian American history and identity, helped create alternative organizations, such as the on-campus food co-op and a day care center, all while being active in student government, in particular its finance committee.

In the summer of 1971, I spent two weeks visiting relatives in Hong Kong, six weeks studying Mandarin in Taiwan, then four weeks hitching the highways of California visiting Asian American studies programs in the University of California colleges and various communities and community organizations.

Who was I, growing up in the backroom of a laundry in 1950s Queens, New York? The space was so cramped we only had folding furniture: chairs and table by day, and beds by night.

Who was I, cold and hungry because my father gambled away his earnings and my mother raged while trying to feed four small children and keep them clothed? I remember running to school in the snow, in ankle socks, with holes in my shoes, and eating meals of white rice flavored by Campbell's soup and a bit of SPAM.

Who was I, who couldn't go into the homes of classmates and fellow church members because they were white and I was not? The minister witnessing my isolation took me aside and apologized for the behavior of the congregation that paid his salary, but in the 1960s before President Kennedy's assassination, that was the way things were. With a sad smile he said, "Maybe some day things will change. Let's hope."

Who was I, told by my fourth grade teacher, who laughed at me when I said I was trying to write a poem, and said in front of all my classmates, "You'll never write poetry! How can you write poetry?"

Who was I, constantly admonished by my grandmother for being a girl and not a boy? And compared to my two younger sisters, to be an ugly girl at that...so dark, so tall, so bony.

Who was I, this solemn, dark-eyed, long-haired, straight-backed girl in the starched, white Peter Pan collared blouse and navy blue jumper?

Who was I?

* * *

I imagined myself a Native American walking erect, proud and self suf-ficient. Didn't I look like an Indian? From the storybooks at the local public library, they were the only people who looked like me.

With shiny black hair to my waist in braids or loose, dark almond shaped eyes, I was strong, swift and lean living within the world: the stars, moon and sun, the flowing rivers and oceans, trees soaring in the forest.

At ease with the universe, I knew how to fish and hunt, to cure skins and make clothing; build shelters from branches and mud; knew what plants to eat, berries to pick, grains and nuts to store in the changing season; to preserve enough food through cold winter until the Chinook wind came east and signaled spring.

I made bowls from the earth and fired them in the ground; made musi-cal, ceremonial instruments and masks in celebration of life and the passages of time; I knew life to be wonder-filled, mysterious each new day.

This was my talisman: the vision of who I was in this life. I wore it like a magical charm on a necklace as I moved in the world that was real, that had jagged, harsh, sometimes hurtful and painful edges. I believed like some Native American warrior princess that I had all that I needed in wits, strength, spirit and passion to deal with whatever came my way.

MRS. HO

Sitting at Anna's kitchen table in cold, rainy Munich, I'm enjoying the warmth of her kitchen after too many nights in *pensiones* in Italy catching train connections to small border towns. Last fall was a time of transition and I had to leave the city again with all my belongings in one bag, a phrase book and a roundtrip ticket.

Anna is in the midst of packing up her storefront apartment filled with too many memories of times and people past. She moved here eight years ago with a collective of friends and they ran a youth and cultural center for street kids. She shows me photographs of the young people, some who stop by now to help her pack. "The landlord raised the rent from 500 DM to 1500 DM," Anna says.

Connie and Evert have come to take the kitchen cabinets. They were part of the collective and live two doors down. Next spring, they too will leave Georgenschwaig Strasse and move to a farm owned by Connie's parents in Bavaria, away from the eerie lights of the BMW factory.

Maria calls and says we must have tea and cakes before I leave for Zurich on Saturday for the flight home. She will bring Lucie, her fifteen month old, and we will visit the park called the Shit-pile, which was land-filled with bricks from the bombed out buildings from World War II.

I look at the bananas on the table and remember the story Anna and Maria told me about Chernobyl. Munich city officials informed its citizens about the radioactive fog drifting through the city the day after it had passed. At the time Anna and her friends were having a picnic in the park. They tell me, "Do not sit on the stoop, because the concrete is radioactive. At the greengrocers buy only fruits and vegetables from New Zealand, Chile and Australia." Parents were outraged when they learned the sandboxes the children were playing in had not been refilled, but merely sifted over. There is fear for the children's futures.

Anna comes into the kitchen. "Fay, meet Mrs. Ho." Mrs. Ho enters with a bag of shrimp chips and sits down for a chat. She is thirty one and lived in Berlin with her family. They left Hong Kong when she was fifteen and then she married Mr. Ho, who is much older and runs the Chinese restaurant a few doors away. Mrs. Ho is the cook.

"There are very few Chinese people in Munchen. I can't cook correctly. We can't get the right ingredients. Usually supplies come from London's Chinatown, but it is very expensive. Come over for a bowl of 'bok fan'— white rice—and try my cooking. It is not too good."

We are speaking Cantonese. Anna comes in and speaks German with Mrs. Ho and English with me. The three of us are bilingual in some combination of Chinese, German and English.

I think of home and the streets of New York Chinatown. In the Chinese restaurant in Rome by the Termini, the waitress yelled to the cook that the order was for a 'hong yen' or Han Chinese person and the meal was cooked family style. It was nothing fancy: a pot of jasmine tea, chicken and vegetables with a steaming bowl of rice, chopsticks and a bottle of soy sauce.

Mrs. Ho says, "My daughter is ten and we live in the apartment across the street over the bakery. Have you been to London? I hear the Chinatown there has many buildings, stores and restaurants. I've even met some Chinese people from Australia! I want to learn English, but Mr. Ho says it's not important. He's been to London and New York Chinatown. He had a good time. I have not left Germany since we came here. My parents live with us and we do all the work. We save money by not hiring workers. It is hard. It is only a small restaurant, but a lot of work."

I feel as though I were talking to my mother's younger self here in Anna's kitchen in Munich. Mrs. Ho's voice is wistful, her hands rough with work. She dreams of distant places. But she is tied here to parents, husband and child as the dutiful daughter, wife and mother. Within me I hear screaming, a wrestling and tearing of flesh: What do we take? What do we leave behind? Whose lives do we live? What dreams do we hold tight?

For now, Mrs. Ho and I smile across the table and have shrimp chips with tea.

MRS. OLTRANI

"Biera? Mangera?" Mrs. Oltrani asks. She invites me into her dining room and we have a glass of beer together. Her TV is blasting a re-run of StarTrek dubbed in Italian. This is my second night in her apartment.

I arrived here at Santa Margherita Ligure on the Italian Riviera by train with all my possessions in a daypack. I was in another period of transition and in another country. I quickly found all the rooms *"completo"*. Mary, a graduate student from UC Santa Barbara, spied me on the street staring into a guidebook. She asked me if I needed help, in English. We walked towards her *pensione*. The woman of the house said there would be a wait of three days.

The guidebook instructed, "If all else fails, get thee to a nunnery." Mary said, "I think it's on the street parallel to this one, because I can see a whole group of nuns from my balcony. In the evening, they work in the garden."

We climb the steps leading to the convent door. A nun appears at a second story window and asks us what we want. Mary explains in Italian that I am looking for a room. The nun disappears and reappears with a scrap of paper. She throws it towards us. Floating like a leaf, it lights on my hand. It reads:

"See Mrs. Oltrani at Via Roma 45."

We find our way to a courtyard next to the train station. A neighbor points out the building and we enter an apartment on the fourth floor. Without question, Mrs. Oltrani hands me a set of keys and smiles, *"Mangera?"* *"Grazie, non."* Mary and I head out for a café.

The next morning, Mrs. Oltrani gives me a beach towel. *Ascugiamano per spiaggi.* I hear her waking up at 7:30 A.M. and taking her first puffs on a cigarette and a nip from the cupboard. We smile and nod, *"Bon giorno."*

I sleep in a large bedroom and wonder if this is hers. There is a large wardrobe and dresser and the *letto matrimonale*. From the window I can see balconies of other apartments, kitchens; people walking in and out of the courtyard. Below, there is a dog pacing his balcony. When I call out, "Hey!" it wags its tail. I smell the flowers from the garden and feel a sense of home. I've spent too many nights in spare *pensione* rooms. Here I smell lunch cooking by the woman who comes in at noon with groceries and does the housework.

"*Freda,*" Mrs. Oltrani has put my fruits into her refrigerator. I leave the door open and she looks in while I am writing. "*Studante?*" "*Non, poeta.*" "*Si, si.*"

Tonight I show her my books of poetry and a copy of the Basement Workshop Yearbook, the nonprofit Asian American arts organization I had recently closed after running it for twelve years. The familiar faces stare at Mrs. Oltrani and me as we turn the pages. We try a little French.

> "*Mes amis sont les artistes and les ecrivains. J'ai deux soeurs. Et la, ma sorella et le filo de ma sorella.*"
>
> "*Et lei? Solo?*"   "*Si.*"
>
> "*Si? Quanto annes ha?*"   "*Trente quatro.*"
>
> "*Tsk! Tsk! Tsk! Io...settanta.*"

"Seventy," I say and nod. Somehow through pantomime, dictionary, fingers and wild gesturing, I learn her husband has died, she is alone; her son is married and has a family. We look at photographs of her grandchildren and extended family. Her younger daughter studied at the University in Rome and lives there with her family. We get teary eyed over beer. She is frail, about four feet ten inches and says her leg is a problem. She points to her cane.

I look at her seated at this large dining room table meant for six and the couch where she now sleeps. The wine glasses and liquor glisten in the cupboard next to her friend the television.

She asks me if I like Italy and where I will go after her town by the sea. "*Andare a Roma a Vaticano.*" I wonder if she has been to Rome. Trains passing rattle the house, their whistles disappearing into the night.

In the room next to mine lives a family of three: father, mother and little girl. The father leaves at 6 A.M. for work. His work pants dry on a wash line over the tub. *"Per famille di poverte,"* Mrs. Oltrani says. A pious old woman opens her home to women traveling alone and poor families trying to make their way with her generous acts of charity, acts of faith.

I think of my mother in the laundry listening to the Chinese radio station while doing her ironing, her work broken now and then by customers who pick up their brown paper packages of clean laundry tied with white string. She cooks simple meals with rice, dishes learned from the China of her childhood. Now she only cooks for herself and Bobo, our family dog of thirteen years. Even Bobo has had an operation and no longer escapes into the streets looking for mischief.

Upstairs is the family apartment with the artifacts of our family history. Photo albums line the bookcase my father brought home from the Salvation Army. Its glass panes we polished every Saturday of our childhoods. And in the kitchen, the table that once seated six. Sunday mornings my father flipped pancakes over the stove and my mother squeezed fresh orange juice. We four kids sat around like hungry pups. The furniture pieces were old friends we used as trampolines. The porcelain gods of compassion and longevity smiled from their shelves. My mother placed three fresh oranges in a bowl at their feet and lit sticks of fragrant incense. On the walls were embroidered pictures of birds and flowers, calligraphy running up and down their sides.

In this room, we sat at the big dining room table doing homework, watching TV, and practiced writing calligraphy for our Chinese classes on Sunday at the Chinese School on Mott Street in Chinatown. Here, we also cursed the embroidery, knitting, crocheting and sewing projects my mother concocted in her attempts to turn us into skilled home-makers. We, three sisters, were proper when guests came to visit. We poured tea, served tea with both hands respectfully holding the teacups towards the guests and made polite conversation in soft voices.

At night we sang songs till we could not stay awake or we would take turns telling ghost stories. Here, I lay awake and watched the flickering shadows from headlights of passing cars playing on the walls of our room. In the warmer weather, the big kids drag-raced their cars on the main street, their laughter and radios cutting through the night air thick with the scent of mimosa and honeysuckles. My parents muttered—loud enough so we could hear—terrible endings for these undisciplined children. They sat in the kitchen reading the Chinese newspaper and having their nightly cup of tea.

The telephone rings. It is Mrs. Oltrani's son. He calls her every night. *"Andare a Roma. Mangera in camera. Si. Spiaggi. Poeta."* She is talking about me.

Two days later at noon I am getting ready to leave for Rome. I've packed and make a last entry about Santa Margherita di Ligure into my journal. Mrs. Oltrani comes in and says, *"Andare in Christo. Andare in pace."* We hug. I say, *"A Vaticano, io* (then make a prayerful gesture with my hands, not knowing the word 'to pray') *per lei."* Mrs. Oltrani bursts into tears and sobs into my neck because her husband is gone, her children gone, her bad leg, her illness. *"Solo, solo, solo."* We are women alone.

We kiss each other on both cheeks and smile. She wipes away her tears. *"Mangera?" "Grazie, non."* She blows her nose and walks into her kitchen coming back with a huge salami. *"Per Roma,"* she says. *"Non, non, grazie."* I show her my bag of cheese and bread and ham. *"Si, si, fromaggi, panna, cotto. Si, si."* On the TV, an American game show is dubbed in Italian. We take each other's photos and she gives me her address. *"Ecco, retourno a Italia, ecco, in mia casa." "Molte grazie, Signora."* Leaving the courtyard I turn and look up towards the fourth floor. Mrs. Oltrani is waving good bye.

In St. Peter's Basilica by the bronze statue of St. Peter with the toe worn thin by the touches and kisses of pilgrims, I too touch the toe and think of Mrs. Oltrani sitting at her dining room table, her cane leaning against a chair, having a smoke and a glass of beer, the TV turned on.

Andare in pace.

CHINATOWN

I first saw you
   through a window
   my forehead pressed
   against glass pane

The small village of Chinatown
early 1950s
New York City

The family shirt-pressing factory
failed in the shadows
of the El in Jackson Heights.
My mother, baby sister and I were banished
to Chinatown while
Dad struggled to start up a hand laundry

In a fourth floor walk-up on Bayard Street
two rooms in a row
toilets in the hallway   no tub
I played with neighbor kids running
the length of dark, dank hallways

Broken immigrant families
fathers at work in restaurants and laundries
scattered over five boroughs
Connecticut, New Jersey
up and down the East coast as far as Boston
or the Midwest and Chicago

Mothers sewed piecework at home
strung plastic jewelry
on kitchen tables;
children making a game of the work
that would feed them

Families made do with weekly
monthly or no visits
Families who were used to

communal dinners and feast days
entire villages celebrating
Lunar New Year
thirty days of laughter
visiting and eating
parades and fireworks
Generations of family
and friends whose lives were
interwoven into
an unspoken promise
of kinship

Here, in *"gum san"*/ "Gold Mountain"
with *"fu lic"*/ "bitter strength"
working hands fight time
bent backs defy
weight and
the kind of fatigue
that cuts muscle and spirit

This was a newfound
loneliness
threatening to shroud the heart
isolation
in a foreign land
among strangers

Sometimes I thought
I saw that feeling
its shadows playing games
against walls
on the landings above
or below the stairwell
I heard wind whistling
and howling in
airshafts
fearing
these were the ghosts
of old Chinatown sojourners
wailing lost dreams

wandering
having lost their hopes
and way back home
to China

My mother only left the apartment
with us on errands, visiting
other women friends or
taking us to Columbus Park
in the early 1950s
proper women followed
village customs
were rarely seen on the streets
eyes downcast
surrounded by children
whispers circulating quickly
about those who digressed
in demeanor or dress

We moved from shop to shop
I was intoxicated
smells of garlic and oil
hissed in hot woks
steamed rice
cups of thick coffee and cream
"don hot"/egg tarts or
"don go"/sponge cakes
always the talk in Cantonese
flying over my head
about the latest gossip
and news from "home", China

You haunt me with
your smells and images
men reading Chinese newspapers
in noodle shops, park benches
cigarette smoke rising
from their fingertips
Old Timers
speaking Cantonese dialects--

the poetic, living form of language
whose equivalent would be Latin
to modern English—
Coffee shops named
"Hoy Hong"/Sweet Ocean
"Mei Lai Wah"/"Beautiful China
men playing mahjong in backrooms
of shops lining Mott Street;
carting merchandise
food on hand trucks or
bamboo baskets suspended from poles
cleavers cutting roast duck
and biting the wood block

The women run
delivering or picking up piecework
from factories, shop and haggle
over the price, over pennies,
over fruit, vegetables, meat
piecing a meal together

Women carrying babies
tied to their backs with red silk
cloths embroidered with
floral patterns and the character
"Hay"/Happiness
Babies who were precious
and rare in Chinatown's
Bachelor Society
immigration laws having restricted
the flow of women and children
since 1882
only allowing men into the country
making use of their cheap labor

These images still live on
in your streets
I pace them
their names imprinted
in my heart

Bayard, Mott, Pell,
Doyer, Bowery, Mulberry
Canal, Division, Orchard,
East Broadway, Henry,
Catherine.
All hours of the day and night
I have walked these streets
memories
coursing through my veins
I hold onto them
like charms

a child's wish
that they will
make sense
some day

GRANDMA

When we moved to the backroom of a laundry in Jackson Heights, Queens when I was almost three years old, we were told not to play with those *"lofan si lo gor"* or children of the "foreign devils." They tossed rocks at us and beat us up with tree limbs yelling, "Chink, chink, chink!"

Until the day my mother's mother came to visit us from Chinatown. We were walking around the block admiring the gardens and flowers of these semi-detached Archie Bunker pre-war houses one mile away from LaGuardia airport. The kids started taunting us and one boy came at us with a stick.

My five foot garment working grandmother snatched that stick and broke it in half, threw it on the ground and started cursing quickly and loudly in Cantonese, "Dead bone head! Useless bastard! Your parents should drop dead for not knowing how to raise you! Come here! Come here! I'll give you a blow to your head! Dead snakes! The whole bunch of you, dead snakes!"

It was marvelous. My parents had instructed us not to confront these kids. If they taunted us, we were to run back to the safety of the laundry, where my father's face would peer from the storefront window. "We need their parent's business, so we may have rice to eat. Do not yell at the children and do not hit them."

"Moy bei yen da nay!" my grandmother instructed loudly as she glared at the backs of the kids disappearing around the corner. "Don't let anyone hit you!" Kicking the sticks, she added with a sharp look at us, *"Mo ng gei duk."*

Don't forget. We continued our walk, admiring the peaches and apples hanging in other people's gardens.

EATING BAO-TZES   *Journal Entry   February 23, 2007*

Came back to New York Chinatown on the Flushing Chinatown van eating fried bao-tzes. I sat in the back row behind a mother and her little two year old daughter who was so delighted by the speed of the van as it hit the highway, she began yelling, "Hoo, hoo, hoo!" over and over again, to the smiles of all those sitting around her.

Yes! I thought. Here are my people, recent immigrants from China, Taiwan, Thailand, Southeast Asia, at the end of a work and school day lugging bags of groceries, book bags, shopping, in transit amongst kindred spirits, bypassing the subway system. Here is a living definition of what it means to be Asian American, changing with each generation in the particularities of its time.

Queens in the 1950s meant the isolated existence of my family living in the backroom of a cramped laundry among the larger communities of Irish and Italian Catholic and Jewish American neighbors in East Elmhurst. Ninety-fourth Street was the dividing line between white and black, where the African American community lived, among them Malcolm X, before his home was torched. I remember the night the fire engines streamed into the nearby streets. My father read us the headlines of the Daily News next morning in English, explaining a black leader's family's home had been burned, but they didn't know who did it.

The isolation was so deep and so cutting in the 1960s it propelled us second and third generation Asian Americans from the laundries, factories, Chinatowns, Little Tokyos, concentration camps, the migrant fields to fight for our civil rights, lessons we learned watching the Black communities' leaders murdered, their homes and streets burned and as they rallied to demonstrate for their human rights from the black and white television sets in our homes. We were sick and tired of the postwar hypocrisies of the 1950s.

Struggling for Asian American studies with other ethnic, progressive, gay and women's studies programs across the country, we concurrently participated, organized and began addressing community-based, grassroots needs and issues in health and mental health, voting rights, education, employment, the legal and prison systems, housing, hunger and to end the war in Vietnam.

In the 1970s the group of young artists, writers, cultural and community activists I worked with, like many others from that generation, started community-based and grassroots-run cultural organizations that evolved into institutions which paved the way in the 1980s for individual artists and professionals who began crossing over in growing numbers into corporate art, music, performance, publishing, media, recording industries to either make it, leave it or get broken by it.

How aspects of the immigration experience now is so very familiar, yet very different from generations past. People migrating from Asia come from varying class and educational backgrounds. They have a mobility my parents and grandparents could only dream about, not working only as a laborers or merchants, but arriving to America often-times with a command of English and knowledge of their civil rights. There are more communities to live, work and attend schools throughout NYC or beyond into the far reaches of New Jersey, Pennsylvania, Ohio, Washington, DC, Maryland, Virginia, Tennessee, South and North Carolina, Florida, where families can buy houses and set up businesses; and are actively involved in their communities. Demographics in our country are changing.

And yet it is also the same, as this country's institutions are slow to respond to the greater needs of and at great costs to, its people by pouring resources into wars overseas, benefiting war-mongers and the military industrial complex (the phrase still fits), because there are still many cramped in railroad flats or public housing, no heat no hot water, undocumented and living in fear, who are unemployed or underemployed or losing jobs as the economy falls, no healthcare, lack of social services and children who don't have a chance. This is all Asian America. A loud "Yes!", to the response and to the refrain of *"Si, se puede!"*

Here, in a van full of Asian Americans from all walks of life and all parts of the globe, the future lives in the spirited "Hoo, hoo, hoo!" of a little girl.

ORCHARD STREET

It is winter. My grandmother, her head and shoulders wrapped in a shawl and I, bundled against the chill wind, hurry along the busy streets of Chinatown.

We come to a street full of clothing hanging from awnings, piled on pushcarts. I am five and grandmother wants to buy me a dress for my birthday.

"Here. Eat this. Very good. Made from potatoes." I stare at a bun-shaped steaming something wrapped in coarse brown paper. I take a bite and years later learn it's called a knish.

No one is speaking Chinese, the only language I know until I enter kindergarten. "Watch and you will see what is happening. In your life there will be times you will be in a different country, not know the language. Watch. You will learn all that you need and know what to do."

This is from my five foot grandmother who never learned to read or write Chinese, but left on her own two—unbound—feet from our village in Sunwei, Guangdong and tracked down grandfather and wife number two when they hit the road for Singapore.

Having caught up with them, grandmother hauled grandfather into court. The judge ordered grandfather to take her back into her rightful place as First Wife. Second Wife did not stay longer than a minute and split with another guy. Soon Third Wife joined the family and got along, very well, with grandmother.

My grandmother is bargaining using her fingers and holding dollar bills. She works and earns pennies in the garment factory *"jin sin"*, cutting threads from garments. Sometimes she sleeps overnight on the factory bundles in order to make enough money to feed my young uncles, aunt and grandfather.

She is using that precious money to buy me a dress—a bought dress—instead of making me one from fabric scraps she picks up from the factory floor.

I see that dress: small white polka dots in a field of midnight blue, white collar and buttons; two long sashes that make a pretty bow in the back. We hurry home to help grandfather make dinner for the 30 or so extended family members and friends, who squeezed into that fourth floor tenement apartment on Henry Street every Sunday. Cheeks cold, my hand is warm and held tightly by grandmother.

Orchard Street. I work on that street now in a youth center for young people at risk, Project Reach, 52 years later, more than half a century.

That memory is a frozen snapshot, like all grandmothers with their granddaughters bargaining at the market, walking down dusty roads, traveling on a train: Afghanistan, Iraq, Palestine, Haiti, Spain. Do you see two figures—an older one bent over a younger one--silhouetted against a blast; and the deafening silence that follows.

Chinatown became a ghost town after *that* blast. No one on the streets. No traffic on the bridges. Shops shuttered. Fighter jets zoomed overhead. Jeeps and soldiers with guns stationed at major crossroads: 14th Street, Houston, Grand, Canal, Chatham Square. These were checkpoints where one had to show a photo ID and an address within the zoned district to gain entry.

She began dying then. Chinatown. Trucks that infused her factories with raw materials and foot traffic slowed to a trickle. Food markets and fruit stands closed earlier. People fled to other Chinatowns in Queens and Brooklyn, escaping the overwhelming stench of fire, smoke and decaying human flesh; seeking work to feed their families.

Unemployed fathers and mothers target their despair, battering those closest to them. Their children tell woeful stories; bearing responsibilities too heavy for their young shoulders.

In the stillness, empire builders move in, destroy and steal the rights of others to live. Men and women rounded and locked up in detention centers without recourse, because of their facial features, the color of their skin, their customs and beliefs. Their lives and families ripped apart. Immigrant sidewalk peddlers eking out pennies are harassed by a city wanting pristine streets.

Who profits? Whose terror? Whose security? Who gains from secret done-deals dealt in the shadows of secret meeting places, in the hush of a blast? Whose homeland?

We are betrayed.

Grandmother said, "Watch. Then you will know what to do."

PORTRAITS

Brush laden with black paint strikes the primed white cardboard surface. I trace the outline of a face.

The eyes speak: steadiness, sadness, a lively sense of mischief, humor, openness.

I discover their age by the way skin falls across muscle, bone, nerves; shadows beneath the eyes, furrows on forehead or crinkles at the corners of the eyes. I see tension in the jaw, attitude in the tilt of the head or a grin ready to break into a smile.

These are portraits of young men—the majority young men of color,— killed by the police. I paint several of these each year for the October 22nd Coalition Against Police Brutality's march and rally, where parents, family members and friends bear witness for loved ones whose lives have been stolen. Portraits name the young men and have the dates of when they were killed.

The anger and sadness I feel as I paint these young faces can not be measured against the grief and strength of the families who speak out against the violence wrought upon their own, as though they were animals hunted down by predators.

Young men's lives cut short by the color of their skin and class; schools and educational systems that failed them; living with a hunger of stomach and spirit. Young men killed by being at the wrong place, at the wrong time: Amidou, Nicholas, Silverio, David, Jose, Huang, Fermin, Timur, Jayson, Malcolm, Sean and too many more.

Questions: Why does Homeland Security have the means to hunt down alleged terrorists, but cannot determine how drugs are trafficked and mainlined into the arteries shooting straight into our country's poorest neighborhoods to keep the young doped up, shot up, dead or if alive headed straight into corporate prisons built at rates faster than schools—schools where they would learn enough about the world and their place in it so they would question why things are the way are, where they would gain the skills to challenge social injustices and to want and to work fiercely for social change?

Why are poor young men and women driven into law enforcement or the army risking their own lives; trained not to see that on the other end of the gun is another human being?

Why are the leaders, generals and policymakers not standing at the frontlines of battle themselves or using their own children and grand-children as cannon fodder and chess pieces in games of war for their own gain?

Why?
Why?
Why?

MIDNIGHT BLUE SKY   *A Monologue*

I'm tired. You're right. I have to let go. Lately, I can't sleep. I'm hearing voices. I tell myself these must be bits of monologue, dialogue. My brain is tired.

Did you know last October 2004, I almost walked into the ocean? It was a Sunday, warm for October. It was another period of walking and walking. Nothing was very clear.

This was the third recurrence of the breast cancer since 1994 and five surgeries to date. The last one, in October 2003, the doctors removed my uterus, ovaries and a 20-pound, luckily, non-cancerous fibroid.

A month later my doctor said, "You have tumors in both lungs, your liver. I know you have a young daughter and you may want to get your papers in order. How long? My guess is maybe six months, a year the most. In the meantime, let's try this hormone-inhibitor and see if those tumors won't shrink or at least arrest."

Was this what stage IV breast cancer felt like? Terminal.

Nine months later the drug worked on all the tumors except for one. The doctor said, "This one's aggressive. I know I can't tell you what to do, but I ask you to consider surgery, the removal of the lower lobe of your right lung as soon as possible...and the sooner the better."

I'm so tired. What are the chances that out of a family of six, three of us would come down with cancer? Dad had colon cancer, my brother Peter, Hodgkin's disease, and me with breast cancer. I couldn't make this up!

The more I walked the streets, the more tired I got. I always need to be near water to think clearly. I took the D train to Brighton Beach and started walking along the shore, toward Coney Island.

I am arguing with myself. I've done enough in my life; actually, I've lived several lives and done some good and useful things.

My daughter's older now and the experiment of living with her father that began two years ago is working well, so if I were to pass on, I would have that comforting thought. Staying home with her for the first four years of her life, I see, has helped her become the person she is now: able to know and articulate what her wants and needs are and to make the choices to realize them. Now, as a teenager, she has a vision for her own life, her own future.

All those years of doing poetry readings or workshops here or there, freelance editing in the middle of the night before her 3:00 a.m. nursing and then getting up with her again at 6:00 a.m., counting nickels and dimes to piece together a meal in this sixth floor walk-up with baby, stroller, diaper bag, groceries—the nurturing of the daughter was a gift that forced me to see life with new eyes and opened my heart.

I've been lucky with wonderful friends and I even wrote a poem about how I see my memorial service—quite joyful at the beach in Montauk by the Breakers Motel, Helen and Bob's place, with a big bonfire, guitars playing and singing, food.

I'm not sure I can go through this again: another operation, cutting off another part of my body. On the surface, I look like a whole person, but I'm really pieced together with so many stitches and scars.

Here I was pacing, pacing the beach. The sun was beginning to set. Heading toward the Coney Island my dad loved so much in his youth, fresh from China, on his days off from the grueling laundry work with his cousin Paul and their pal, Bing. He always talked about Nathan's hot-dogs and French fries, skee-ball, riding the roller coaster, learning to swim.

I passed a few families packing up blankets, a man walking his dog, kids flying kites laughing in the wind, an older couple walking arm and arm, seagulls swooping in the air. Everyone was speaking Russian. I thought that through the years the communities changed from Italian, Irish, Chinese, African American, Puerto Rican, Caribbean to now, Russian families. Each wave of newly arrived immigrants gracing these shores, the cold steel blue Atlantic, would settle and fiercely claim the city as its own.

I remembered how our family used to gather on Sundays here on this very beach. The relatives taking a day off from the sewing factories, restaurants and shirt press factories. We brought brown shopping bags carrying homemade sandwiches and dishes, drinks, oranges. Uncle Andy, grandpa's oldest brother, taking us into Washington Square Pool on the boardwalk, the smell of the salt air, amusement rides and games and Dad swinging me into the waves.

I realize: change. The operation would be another transition, another change. I could do that. I've done that before, many times.

Feeling much lighter, I walked toward the boardwalk. Kids were still playing volleyball, their shadows long on the sand, while others strolled into the sunset, a golden, fiery, orange ball against a liquid midnight blue sky.

FLIGHT

For Miki and Xian

They bind us
to this earth

We imagine
flying
like dolls and puppets

from buildings   a missile plummeting through
a canyon of air
over sides of bridges   breaking sheets of blue gray
water

how we
study too intently
cold metal tracks
lights
subway cars
hurtling
towards us
from dark, echoing
tunnels

we stop
our footsteps arrested

your wife/your lifeline   my daughter/my lifeline
crosses continents   swims
oceans   in the ocean of my womb
with you   crosses continents through me
in this   into this
life's journey   life's journey
through the universe   and universe

Their love binds us to this earth
details of living
in an intimate world

we hold dearly

the call towards flight
becomes a whisper

DAVID

I knew him for 3 weeks, 2 days. Nine days face to face. When he was moved to the hospice his family asked me to return for his last days in this life.

When we first meet, he picks us up from San Diego airport, his stomach, ankles and calves swollen, face flinching in pain. In a codeine haze he insists on driving us to his sister's family's home, where he and his elderly mother live.

The prior two weeks he has lain in bed in the dark in great pain, not moving, not eating. His family asks him what would give him ease in this situation. He wants his boyhood friend, John, in New York City to visit him. John and his wife Jamie ask me to accompany John to California to help his friend.

I feel inept. What did I know about San Diego? Who were these people? How did I get myself into this? I don't even drive!

I had to trust the love that John and Jamie had for this friend and their trust in me to be able to help him. He and John had grown up together on the Street of Embassies in Rangoon, across from the University, where as young men they played music in the warm evenings catching the attention of young women students locked up for the night in their dorms.

"We shared everything: food, drugs and needles. Thirty of us. Bored. We had nothing to do, no jobs, no where to go. Every night five bands played rock and roll until the sun rose. We had good times! And now everyone is dead. AIDS. Only the two of us survived. Now the only friend, who can share my memories, is sick."

We get to the house late on Monday, Presidents Day. Everything is closed. No information. I call John Manzon, the executive director of API Wellness Program in San Francisco for a contact. He refers me to the Asian Pacific Islander Community AIDS Project or APICAP, promising to call Jess San Roque, the executive director, to help us.

What can I do to turn this situation around in four days? We are scheduled to fly back to New York on Saturday at 6 AM. How can we bring relief to David's pain and suffering? Give him hope? What resources and support are available?

As I observe and listen, I feel David has been robbed of his personhood. He and his mother live in the house taking care of chores, cooking, driving, cleaning—isolated, overwhelmed. Not complaining, earning their keep, grateful.

In the few days we are there, we find the people who came to love him. At APICAP, Maria, Elmer, Jess welcome David into a community of people living with AIDS, a place that becomes home. They help him apply for entitlements, fill out paperwork and suggest we visit the Owen Clinic of UCSD Medical Center, which specializes in working with people living with AIDS with liver conditions.

At the Lesbian, Gay, Bisexual, Transgender Center, Carrie, the psychologist, also tells David to go to the Owen Clinic. She gently suggests he visit the San Diego Hospice. "See the place and resources. I'm not saying you need it now, but it's something you can think about for the future."

The next day is Wednesday. David and John wonder, "Can we just walk into the Owen Clinic without an appointment?" I say, "We can walk into any place and ask for information." We are informed they have no appointments for another two weeks. I say to the receptionist, "My cousin (everyone becomes my cousin, brother, family member so the medical professionals will speak to me) here is doubled over in pain and swollen in his stomach and ankles and I have flown here having just had half my right lung removed from my fourth bout of breast cancer six weeks ago. We're exhausted. We're in pain. Someone has to help us. My other cousin, John, here and I have to fly back to NYC Saturday at 6 AM."

We are given an appointment for Friday at 1 PM.

We tour the hospice set on a hill. The buildings look like Japanese temples and are quiet and serene. Each room has a hospital bed, a fold out sofa for family members, TV/Video unit, bathroom and an expansive view of landscaped grounds and blossoming trees. David is very sad.

I feel he needs new memories, no matter how short the number of days he has left in this life. At one point I ask John to stop talking about the past, their youth on those warm, muggy, music-filled nights in Rangoon. You need a present and a future to be able to look at the past.

In the car with John driving, David's navigating and I'm in the back seat with pathology and lab reports prepping for the next appointment, windows wide open, wind blowing and the clouds billowing in electric blue skies after morning rains, the radio blasting oldies. For this moment we are tight friends burning miles down those southern California highways.

We eat late lunches at Vietnamese, Japanese and touristy fish restaurants by the water. Make pit stops in gas stations, Starbucks and Baskin-Robbins for ice cream cones, stops in pharmacies, the post office to overnight birthday cards to Jamie in New York City, shop at mega-Asian supermarkets for ingredients for the night's dinner.

After a tiring day of appointments, we eat big meals late at night prepared by David's mother while she tells us more stories about their boyhood. David and John sit at the dining room table like two teenaged best friends delighted to be in each other's company again, giggling; delighted to be eating their favorite dishes prepared by a mother's loving hands.

Then David lies down on the sofa, cushioned amongst pillows, covered in blankets waiting for the codeine to ease his pain. Two evenings John and I sing the old songs he requests. "A Little Help From My Friends," "Help!", "Crazy Little Thing Called Love", "Proud Mary", "It Never Rains in Southern California", "Peaceful, Easy Feeling".

"I would have died in my room if you hadn't come to San Diego."

Thursday we see his primary care physician who explains his treatment plan for David. He has stabilized David's HIV/AIDS, then his high blood pressure, diabetes and cholesterol. He was in the process of getting David into a clinical trial for Interferon, when spots were detected on his liver CAT-scan, suggesting liver cancer was present which made him ineligible for clinical trials.

"Why was he not given Interferon when the liver specialist suggested that four years ago when he was first diagnosed with Hepatitis C? Four years ago?" The doctor says he has done his best for David medically. "Why was he not referred to the Owen Clinic? Why does he only have county medical insurance, when as a permanent resident, he was eligible for MediCal, Social Security Insurance, Food Stamps, Section 8 housing?" He says, "That is not my job." I ask, "Whose job is it?" and he replies, "It's the social worker's job."

The doctor says before he leaves the examination room, "I'm sorry."

I want to hit him in the knees with a lead pipe.

How did this happen? How could David be in this condition? His viral load is undetectable, but here he has liver failure when all the resources he needs for treatment are available in the city he lives in? Why this lapse of communication between doctor and social worker? Where is his family in all of this? Why is everyone in such denial in the face of his pain? Why is he silenced and shamed, living in the dark? Are the doctors on burn-out? People are building careers-- within the HIV/AIDS industry-- on the pain of the people they are supposed to be serving.

David says, "I treat the nurses and doctors so good. Every Christmas I write a card and bring cookies and a good bottle of wine to show my appreciation. I had hoped they would look out for me."

John says, "Brother, in this country you have to be direct and tell people what you need, what you want. If they do not hear you, talk louder; say it in different ways until they understand what you are asking them to do for you. It is their job. This is not Asia where you must be so polite, so indirect. This is America and you have to be direct, make people see you."

Friday morning we go to Costco. David buys presents to thank all the people he has met these past three days. We deliver cookies to APICAP and they admire the beautiful orchid. We sit and share a meal with staff and clients at the weekly community potluck lunch. David eats with gusto. This will be the last meal he has that is not in the hospital or hospice, although in that moment we do not know this.

In the afternoon at the Owen Clinic, Dr. Campbell assesses and tells David that he needs to be admitted to the main hospital in order to expedite tests that would determine exactly what is causing his pain; to manage the pain; hydrate, nourish and strengthen him; so he could rest.

He weeps. I am waiting with him in the ER for a bed to be prepared upstairs. "Look at me. My mother always told me to study. We were young. Music. Drugs. I should have listened to her." He talks about his parents, siblings, the excitement of coming to and making a new life in America, working and then the virus debilitating him. I say, "Day by day. Focus. Save your strength."

He wants morphine.

In his hospital bed drowsy with painkillers, his family, John and I say goodnight. I leave my prayer beads with him, wrapped three times in his fist and tell him how the fragrance from the sandalwood beads helped me sleep during my last two surgeries.

John and I catch a 6 AM flight back to New York. I feel I have left many things undone. During the intervening two weeks, I call David, his family members, his team of doctors, nurses, case managers, social workers; have pathology and test reports faxed over, once, two or three times a day; check to see that his MediCal application is submitted so he won't feel like he is a financial burden to his family; that he is paying his own way. His family says he tells them, "Don't worry. Fay will take care of everything."

When I return to San Diego, David has such a big smile when I walk into his hospice room. He and his family calls me his angel in New York City. I am filled with rage: if I had only met him six months earlier when his liver was still okay, this wouldn't be happening. I have no place to put these messy feelings and thoughts and feel crazy, while I sit in a chair in the corner as many visitors fill the room.

"He doesn't have a cousin in New York City," a woman my age accuses me in English. I explain by claiming to be a relative, the doctors will speak with me. "What's wrong with David? Why wasn't this liver cancer taken care of earlier?" The family asks me not to mention AIDS. Their community does not know. To distract her, I go into great detail about my six surgeries dealing with breast cancer in the past eleven years. She is horrified.

Maria, a case manager, from APICAP visits in the evening. David asks, *"Do you speak Spanish?"* "Of course I do! I was born in Mexico." *"Can you take Fay to Tijuana? In her two visits here she has only seen doctors and hospitals. If she went by herself, people would call her Chinita, but with you speaking Spanish it would be okay."* Maria says, "So I should take Fay to Tijuana?" *"Yeah."* "I have your permission?" *"Yeah."* Surprised I say, "Okay. I'll go. I've never been to Tijuana."

His sister and I stay for the next three days and nights in the hospice with David. Soon he cannot speak, but can hear and see. The morning of his passing he wakes up at 5, looks at his sister and me. Smiles. Then fights like hell and tears his tubes and clothing off. The nurse gives him a relaxant and he falls into a deep sleep. Roger, the nurse practitioner, shines a flashlight into his eyes. No response. His extremities are cold. Roger says, "Soon his work here will be done." David's breathing grows weaker and weaker and then stops. There is a peaceful smile on his face.

That afternoon Maria and I drive to the border half an hour away by car into Tijuana. We have a plate of tacos at a roadside stand, El Gordo Tacos; cross the road to a coconut stand and toast David and the passing of his spirit with fresh coconut juice. We feel surely he is still and will always be with us, because he has touched us so deeply.

He passed away a week ago. I have to let go of this anger and frustration. I think David felt we had prolonged his life, changed the quality and color of it, the way he saw his own self; that his new friends cared and loved him; that it did not matter he was living with HIV/AIDS.

He is part of a community and he is not alone.

DIVING

For Moe

You tell me,
    With our illnesses
        we are ones
    who have crashed
      to the bottom;
    there is no more
        below.
   You see, the only way
      is up

Like diving, I say,
   diving for pearls
     we are immersed in
        velvet waters
      sinking towards
      silent
     dark ocean floor
       amongst rock,
         seaweed, sea life
     pulling crusty
       oysters, our
         breaths strained
           until we must
      hurl our bodies
     skyward
   for air, for light

Not all oysters
   have pearls.

That does not stop us,
  from diving
     or trying again,
   and again
     and again

Isn't that found pearl
   most
    precious

CHEE

For Letitia, Yongyoot, Michael, Sidd, Mary and Don

Chee passed away yesterday, Sunday, afternoon very peacefully at home. I got to his apartment around noon and sat by his bedside holding his hand. He was looking out the window. Rolling clouds shaped like dragons raced across a sunlit blue sky. Chee and I are both Aquarian dragons.

****

"I've never been to the Farm", he says in April, a short two months ago. We check with Dr. Johnson who says, "Take him" when we tell her it's only two hours by car into the Catskills. Michael flies in from San Antonio thanks to Mary's frequent flyer miles and we all pack food, sleeping bags and gear into Don's van and head north to his family's retreat space.

Letitia and Yongyoot cook up a storm: steak and mushrooms, curry chicken, satay noodles, the rich aromas filling the farmhouse mixed with storytelling, gossip and a song here and there. Chee doesn't want to go to bed and stays up till dawn. Both nights he tells travel stories in a strong voice while snacking away. He loves to eat. He is too weak to walk outside until the very last day.

With our canes we walk slowly down to the creek a few yards from the porch and he keeps talking about his next doctor's appointment until I ask him if he wants me to go with him. *Why? Are there things you want to ask her?* I say, No, do you want to ask her anything yourself? *Maybe to see what is next in my treatment.* Okay, I'll go with you.

On the way home we all sing happily along to Don's tape of oldie songs...off-key, of course. He wears the long scarf of white yarn speckled in black, grey, maroon and beige he asked me to crochet for him, wrapped several times around his neck and shoulders for warmth.

****

.

Around 3:30 PM, this might sound strange but I feel a chemical or electrical charge between the palms of our hands. His breathing becomes less difficult, slower. When I move my hand out of his, he squeezes it. I remain sitting next to the bed thinking he wants company during this part of his journey.

Letitia and Michael had stayed overnight from Saturday into Sunday with him and the home attendant. When Chee realizes he would have many visitors on Sunday, he insists on getting bathed and shaved. He wants a fresh shirt and changes out of the hoodie he's worn since coming home from St. Vincent's Hospital late Friday afternoon when he says, "Fay! I want to eat two scrambled eggs with butter and toast now! Right now! I'm tired of hospital food!" Then he falls into a contented nap on his leather sofa among his many beloved mementos from his travels around the world in the days he was a tour guide.

Yongyoot arrives and starts cooking in the kitchen, and when he throws fresh garlic into the hot oil in the frying pan and the apartment fills with the aroma of sizzling garlic, Chee cries. Tears fall from the corners of his eyes. Around 4:30 PM, he turns from the window and looks at the photo of himself and his friend, the one above the television. At that moment they are in their mid twenties and they look into the camera with so much excitement, so much life.

Then his spirit leaves.

DREAM

I had the strangest dream early this morning. A dachshund wearing a cone shaped party hat and a starched white Elizabethan ruffled collar around its neck is prancing on its hind legs.

Next to the dachshund a friendly-looking clown juggles three colorful balls and another clown twirls three hula hoops around wrists and waist.

Downstage center a tightrope is suspended about four feet above the ground.

Cut to wide angle shot of this scene and I am walking slowly across this tightrope.

POV: I am looking down at my feet taking small measured steps.

There's circus music, gentle not garish, playing; and then I hear the voice in my head say:
> "A mastery of grace."

TALL GRASSES RIPPLING IN THE WIND

For Peter (1958 to 1982)

Tall grasses rippling in the wind
sun melting fog
I see the ocean from
    the kitchen window
      past tomatoes
      fallen off the vine
        too soon
          on a ledge.

Everyone is sleeping still.

On the sundeck
    I see the road
    going off towards
    the freshwater pond
    birds swooping in arcs
    disappear into rushes
      their calls breaking
      early morning chill.
    The lighthouse beckons.

Slipping away from the house
    I pick mint leaves
      for tea.
By the pond
    sidestepping poison ivy
     I reach beyond brambles
    for blueberries
      covered in dew.
The ocean sings
    undecipherable tunes;
     she leaves her night's treasures
    along the shore:
      small crabs, hermit shells,
      stones glistening,
      broken bits of this and that,
    I gather these too.

Yesterday morning
    in a torrent of rain,
    rush hour traffic,
    horns blaring,
    pedestrians running for shelter,
I left the city.

Mary choreographs
    this exodus of bags
    and groceries,
    connections for trains and ferries.
She tells me,
    "Myron and Regina
        will meet us at the dock."

I think:
    "Peter, you will never see this.
        I cannot tell you about it."

I want to say:
Remember in '71,
        outside of San Francisco
        at Stinson Beach,
        you drag clumps of seaweed
        onto the shore
        and you hold it
        the way fishermen
        hold a prized catch.

Riding down highway # 1,
        we stop and stare into the ocean,
        watch seals calling
        their young,
        and walk among
        that stretch of
        small yellow wildflowers
        shining by a footbridge.

We relish our new freedom
        away from the city,

the family. Here,
we discover we are not
only siblings,
but friends.

We swap stories:
        how you had arrived
        a few weeks earlier
        staying with our relatives,
        you've already seen the sights
        and wandered the streets
                of San Francisco.
        I tell you
                about my weeks in
                Hong Kong and Taiwan,
                my hunger for a taste of pizza!

That summer
        we were riders
        of the roads and highways:
        I hitch up and down
        the coast, back of farm trucks;
        you whet your thirst
        for bus trips cross country.

Or in '78,
        gazing at the Mojave Desert
        at sunset, we gather
        stones with Jean.
        John and Arlene show us
        the fault line
        we touch with our toes.
        Imagine, we said, California
        floating away
        into the Pacific!
        Watching the sky turn fiery orange,
        a cool, calm blue descending
        changes the valley.
        Dark megaliths jut
        from the earth.

You call me
    3 AM and talk
    from a placeless
    phone booth
    taut with love/hate,
    the sorrow and pain
    over our father's death,
    and your own deep pain from
        too many X-rays,
        chemo treatments,
        blood tests, scars,
        operations and
        stays in
        psychiatric wards.

3,000 miles apart
    we grieve over the loss
    of our childhood family
        safe in the back of the laundry
        playing games after public school,
        Chinese school, church and visits
        to grandma and grandpa
        in Chinatown on Sundays
        with Ed Sullivan blasting on
        their living room TV set.

We hold onto
    what we know of each other
    from that time.

I remember the night
you were born.
Ma and Dad went to the hospital
and left me with Jean and Jan.
Barely 6 years old, the eldest
in the back of the laundry
in the middle of the night,
shadows are large.
The sisters are crying.
I said, "They went

to get the baby."
(That was you.)
Jan is 2 years old
and so frightened,
she wets the bed.
I change her diapers,
climb onto a chair,
reach for the candy tin
on top of the refrigerator,
raiding it!
I dole out fistfuls
of M & Ms to my sisters
and glasses of milk.
All in one bed,
they fall asleep.
I wait till Dad
comes home. He asks me
if I am scared.
I just shake my head;
he gives me
a soft pat on the head.

In the morning,
we are awakened
by the doctor's call.
"It's a boy."
Peter, your sisters squeal
and jump on the bed
for joy!

During the first few months,
in the early morning hours
when you cried,
I would crawl out of bed
to feed you, warming a bottle,
burping you and
change your diapers.
Our mother, weak from delivery
has to rest.

Cramped in the back
of that laundry,
10 feet by 14 feet with a
little corridor and kitchen,
our parents raise
the four of us.

You were always mischievous,
    inventing things,
    building go-carts with Jan,
    or setting off firecrackers,
    drawing airplanes,
    building models,
    climbing fences
    with Larry,
    the kid next door,
    riding off on your bikes
    through the back alleys
    of the neighborhood
    or going down to LaGuardia airport
        with your friends Steve and Carlos
        watching planes take off.

A boy, they said. The youngest;
    the only son among three daughters.
    In the silent language
        between fathers and sons
            he taught you the use
            of your hands and mind
            with simple tasks.
            His larger hand over
            your hand curves around
            a hammer feeling its
            weight and force and
            drive against a nail
            biting wood.
    The two of you
            disappear with the dog
            in the evenings,
            go on shopping jaunts

113

to get father-son things,
perhaps the way Dad did
with his father in China.

When you were 14
Dad died.
At the funeral home,
incense and smoke rising
amidst the suffocating
smell of carnations,
we sit huddled in black.
We burn paper money,
bow with incense sticks
in our hands, and
in turn we each spread
a piece of cotton fabric
over our father
lying there in the casket
to keep him warm
on his journey.
The village people murmur
we are to be strong,
not to cry for the sake
of our mother.

You were told
you would now be
the man of the house
for our mother to lean on.

What did that mean?
To be the man of the house?
To be the woman of a house?
A moment ago,
we were kids.
What did this have to do with us?
Especially you
stricken with
Hodgkin's lymphoma
and barely a trace of down
upon your upper lip.

* *

114

Shells lie fragmented in wet sand
    woven by threads of water.
Seaweed floats
    like mesh upon the surf.

Slowly we've walked from the house.
    Mary's foot is in a cast.
    The motorcycle having skid upon sand
    on a ramp leading onto
    the BQE in Brooklyn,
    she was flung
    onto the road.

She tells me,
"A family stops behind us
and the man offers
to take us to the hospital.
An ambulance pulls up
and whisks us to an ER
of a city hospital where
no one knows what's going on
and no one can find the bandages!"

We walk past patches
    of rosehips
    and before descending
    upon the beach
    we settle on the steps
        watching waves
        cap
        thrashing
        like horses
        their hooves
        cutting a path
            through white foam.

We are small in this landscape.

I say:
    Mary, it's like in the movie
    with Marlon Brando,
    "On the Waterfront,"

where he's riding in the cab
with his big brother
and his brother's been ordered
to keep him in line
or snuff him
and he knows it, but
he says to his big brother...

Mary says,
  What are you saying?
  You didn't kill him.
  Your brother was very sick.

  I know, but he says in the movie,
  "I could have been a contender,
  I could have been a some body;
  instead, I was a nobody.
  I thought you were my brother,
  you was going to watch
        out for me..."

Mary says,
  Don't do this to yourself.
  You can't feel guilty
  over something
  you couldn't prevent.
  It was his choice.

  Maybe there was something else...

  Stop.

Shadows grow long.
Sand trickles through my fists.
Gulls circle overhead
    screaming.
The ocean is crashing.
    It is crying.

* *

At the morgue
you look pale
sleeping with your mouth
slightly open,
a sheet drawn over your chest.
A dark blue mark
encircles your neck.
No, this is no longer
you.

I make arrangements
at Wah Wing Sang
funeral parlor on Mulberry Street,
the staff remembering me
from our father's passing;
buy you your first and only suit
slipping on the jacket.
We were the same size
as our father.

I hear the ticking of clocks.
    Healing has its own pace;
    nothing to do with logic;
    we are reminded:
        we are housed in frail bodies,
        breakage resounding loudly.

The house they said
you were the man of
wore at your spirit.
In rage you tore at
its walls wielding
a crowbar shattering
its bowels. Wanting
to torch and burn,
you were grieving
memories of you and Dad
working together,
the loss clutching you.

These rooms graced by our father's
     hands and spirit
     work and life.
These same rooms
     you kept your books,
     and models and records,
     tools and weights,
     guitars and saxophone,
     drawings and writings,
     boxes of teas and grains.
I have packed these away for you.
      They are in the cellar
      by your go-cart and
      the blue toy car
      you peddled up and down
      the sidewalk
      before you began kindergarten.

This house, our father's house
     became cold and empty
     when he died.
Shrill with grief
our mother walks incessantly
the rooms upstairs and
downstairs in the laundry.
She becomes increasingly frightened
      with your cancer
      your spleen surgery
      when both your lungs collapsed
      and each of your
      four hospitalizations
      in psychiatric wards.

Peter, where did you go
      that you left me behind
      this time. I cannot show
      you these seashells.

Last evening at dusk,
      when I was returning

from the garden with tomatoes
and ran into Myron
barbecuing dinner in the front yard
he said,
　　"You have to love
　　the things you need:
　　the ocean, the air and sand,
　　the taste of blueberries
　　and how the birds swoop
　　to drink freshwater
　　from the pond."

I watch Mary crochet a scarf
　growing longer every day.
Regina shows us a new recipe
　and I peddle to the store
　for ingredients.
Mary sets the table balancing
　on crutches.
Myron returns with a bucket
　of blueberries for dessert.
I chop vegetables, mix spices
　over a simmering pot.
The sun has set, the stars glisten.

DAYS END

How shall I end my days?
   My family and friends
   do not want to talk
      about this.
But here,
   this is what I see.

At the end of my days
    when the spirit has moved on
I wish to be cremated
      no traditional wake
     or burial in the custom
       of my ancestors

May my ashes be divided in two:
    the first half to be buried
      in the Sunwei section
      of Cypress Hills Cemetery
        in Queens surrounded by
        my family and friends who
          have passed on:
          over the hill
            my grandfather and grandmother,
            uncle and cousin;
          this side of the hill
            a handful of ashes
            between the side by side
            graves of my father and brother;
         a short distance
            my mother's grave
              under a flowering tree
            put another handful
              of ashes and if
            my family feels compelled,
              a small marker next to
                my mother's tombstone
              with my name in English
                and Chinese
                  my birth and death dates.

My father, brother and mother
  whose wakes and funerals
  I arranged at Wah Wing San Funeral Home
      on Mulberry Street
  where we sat in black
      adorned with black armbands
      and blue woolen florets
          in our hair;
      the smell of incense and
          burning paper money,
          paper houses and paper goods
              carried riches to heaven
              on plumes of smoke
                  rising heavenward.
See the rows and rows
      of floral arrangements
      streamers with names
          and words of sympathy
          written in Chinese calligraphy.
We placed prized possessions
          with the deceased:
              a watch, a favorite pocketbook,
              eyeglasses and items they
                  would need on their journey.
      The crying and mourning,
          closing of the casket
          and movement to the hearse;
      a last ride past the house
          where a relative turned on
          a lamp so the spirit will
                  always know the way home.

The procession rides along the BQE,
          LIE, all the cars with their
          headlights on.
We gather around the grave—
          an open wound upon the earth—
              the casket is lowered,
          we say our sad farewells,
              and toss carnations

        as final prayers
            are said and incense burnt.

    Then the tired drive
            back to a reception
                in Chinatown.

    No. I could not bear this.

Instead,
        I ask for simplicity
        No wake
        No viewing
        No formal burial.

And if we must
        have a memorial for one
        who has arranged and assisted
            in many, let me say
        I would like my memorial
                to take place on my block
                East Fourth Street
        where I have lived
                since 1978
        among neighbors and friends
                whose joys and pains
                we've all shared;
        may I be among them in spirit at
                LaMama ETC
                in a celebration
        of our lives and work
                in the arts.

    If we did not have a chance to speak,
    if we did not see one another
            before this parting
                of the spirit
    let me say,
        "Family and friends,
            remember a time we spent

together, something
we laughed or cried about,
    a photograph or story or
    read some of my poetry!"

In the late spring
    or early autumn
    let us go to the beach
across the Old Montauk Highway
    from the Breakers Motel
    where I've come since 1995,
    the summer after my
            mastectomy.
    It is a place I love
            with many happy memories
            spent with family
                and friends.

Villagers and shopkeepers
    ask after they've seen
        us in all seasons,
    "Why don't you buy a house
    and move out here?"
    A deep and warm measure of
            acceptance in a small, tight
            community of fishermen
                and their families.

Helen, Bob and sons,
    Marley and Lennon, who
    ran the motel always
        welcomed me with warmth,
        meals prepared and eaten
        together. Many cups of tea
    Helen and I sipped at
        the kitchen table sharing
        stories about our lives,
            her jewelry making,
            my writing and art-making,

the nurturing of our
    families, children and selves.

    Toss the rest
      of my ashes
    into the ocean, here.

****

This ocean I have
    known since childhood;
    its steel blue gray waters cold
when our mother brought us
    to Coney Island during
      hot summers by way of
        a bus and two subway lines,
    our lunches, towels and toys
    in bags we carried because
    we never had a car.
Leaving the back of the laundry,
    we came back to our father,
      who had ironed shirts
      all day in the heat,
        for a dinner
    he cooked for his sand-covered,
      tired, but happy children.

This cold Atlantic whose
    waters we saw
    joining the Indian Ocean
    at the Cape of Good Hope
    in South Africa on
    New Year's Day
    during a trip when Xian,
    Mark, Jean and I visited
    Mark's family in
    Johannesburg,
    drove through
      the Drakensburg Mountains,
      Saint John's and Durban,

Pietermartzburg, Knysna,
Port Elizabeth, Muizenberg,
Scarboro, Capetown,
the Karoo, Kimberly
and back to cousin David's
in Jo'burg shortly after
President Nelson Mandela's
victorious election.

At the Cape
the wind was strong along the cliffs,
a whale spouted water
in the distance and baboons
sat in trees staring at
the rising moon in
the parking lot. We waded
along the shore amongst the rocks,
one foot frozen by the
Atlantic, the other warmed
by the Indian Ocean.

Xian, aged five, dressed in a pink
chiffon party dress of her choice,
ribbons flowing
in the wind as she ran up and
down the trail with her cousins
laughing and hugging
in their delight at
meeting one another from
half a world away; yet looking
so much alike—Xian, half Chinese
American and Jewish American;
Roushanna, Satara and Safia,
Javanese ("colored" descended
from four hundred years of
Dutch enslavement) and
South African Jewish. Blood
cousins who vow to meet
again in America or Africa
or any other part of the world—

oh, brave-hearted
adventurous girls!

****

Here in Montauk,
        at the edge
        of sand dunes covered
        with pink dune roses and
        buttercups in early spring,
        honeysuckles and blueberries;.
        in June, wildflowers, lavender,
        mint and the sweet tart
        taste of rosehips' fruit in summer,
        daisies and fields of goldenrod in autumn light
        and snow blanketed dunes of winter
            where I've run headlong into deer,
                rabbits, red foxes among tall grasses,
        watched birds heading south,
        thousands of monarch butterflies
            valiantly migrating towards Mexico
        or stood under moonlight
            watching Haley's comet,
            constellations reflected upon
            mysterious, dark water

I see
    Xian, Sydelle and Dakota running
        ahead with Mark and
        our dogs Nine and Lucky
            their shadows long
            on our winter hikes,
        as I follow more slowly
            retrieving shells, beach glass,
            stones polished by the tides.
        On this beach where we built
            bonfires at dusk
            huddled against chilled
                night air and
            children excitedly roasted

126

marshmallows—smell their
burnt sweetness mingling
with wood smoke.

Here,
let us watch the sunset
share a meal and sing
the old songs, guitars
playing, recite poems
as the moon rises.
There will be—I hear it—
much storytelling and laughter
among families and friends,
children shouting at and
chasing one another
among the dunes or
sleeping in their
mother's and father's arms
wrapped in
sweaters and blankets;
dogs bark in the distance as
the surf crashes against
the shore and stars shine
in a sky of midnight blue.

****

You tell me,
Buddha said,
There is no heaven.

IN THE DIM AFTERNOON LIGHT

for Mine Okubo (1912 to 2001)
and for Kathy Hyde who also loved her dearly.

In the dim afternoon light, the apartment bare, we finally see the fabled marble fireplace. A large mirror emerged, reflecting the ceiling to floor, wall-to-wall windowpanes. A door leading on to the patio lets in the sound of neighbors talking. "The light in New York is just like Parisian light. No wonder the Impressionists lived and worked there," she would tell us.

I imagine her opening this door to this apartment for the first time, fifty-six years ago. Along the graceful, winding staircase up to the third floor in this East Village townhouse, carrying all her belongings in two suitcases and her artwork from Topaz, the concentration camp where she spent the better part of World War II uprooted from her little yellow house on a street corner in Berkeley--paintings, drawings, books, a home, family, friends lost.

Away from the barracks, the desert dust and insects, the sand that was everywhere, the crowded living, bathing, toilet, eating facilities, where no privacy existed.

Away from the extreme heat, the extreme cold, away from the guards in security towers carrying guns.

Away from the barbed wire fences, and a world where one day you were an American citizen, and the next day you were a prisoner of the country of your birth.

A small galley kitchen with a little refrigerator and stove with four burners, cupboards with glass paned doors, an old-fashioned lion claw-footed bathtub deep enough for swimming—the luxury! — as well as a separate hand sink and a tall, tall linen closet. A separate bedroom faced the backyard with its large fragrant fern trees and an oak tree where squirrels ran along black tree limbs and birds built their nests. She watched the seasons here and the ever-changing canvas of open sky day and night.

Can you feel the hopefulness? Can you feel a certain measure of hesitation? Can one begin one's life and career over again? Like a cat. How many lives are we permitted to have in one lifetime?

She who was critically recognized in the 1930s as a young, emerging West Coast artist, for her paintings, drawings and ceramic work in major group and solo exhibitions. Honors and publication— awarded one of Berkeley University's most coveted awards, the Bertha Taussig Traveling Scholarship, to continue her studies in Europe after receiving her master's degree. She studied with Ferdinand Leger in Paris, and was a friend and contemporary of Noguchi; she assisted muralist Diego Rivera as a working artist, and was befriended by his wife, the artist Frieda Kahlo, in the WPA program in San Francisco. Where is all that now?

She hears silence for the first time in many years; and then just the wind, leaves rustling, a bird call, maybe children's voices after school, the aroma of other people's dinners; one's own breathing.

The eyes travel over ceiling, walls, the mantel, fireplace memorizing every surface. Walk to the bedroom. Begin to imagine furniture: an easel, of course, the easel and paints and canvases. Storage already a problem! How about a bed, chairs, a lamp after the sun sets into darkness. Put the suitcases under the windowsill. Make a list: a few cups, dishes, a pot for tea and a frying pan, forks, knives, spoons. Why not Earl Grey tea, milk and sugar for guests and a lemon for one's self? Imagine a lovely embroidered tablecloth on a little round table and linen napkins for visitors. Here, tea biscuits, cheese and fruit.

Plan the day: work through the night, a nap, tea and toast, work from dawn until noon, when all good artists rise and meet for a drink and lunch and errands to the art supply stores New York Central, Del Segn's on 14th Street, browse the secondhand print, map, poster and book-shops along Fourth Avenue, treasure troves of source materials for paintings and illustrations, and then back for cocktails and gossip about who made what deal and who was sleeping with whom with friends at the Cedar Tavern, and more drinks and maybe a museum or gallery opening before a late dinner.

She hosted parties on the patio with Japanese paper lanterns lit by candles under a full moon. Smell the night air filled with the scent of

mimosa and honeysuckle. Food—sushi is a big hit with New Yorkers!—
and more drinks for artist friends but not too late. She must chase out
the ones who linger. In the silence of the night a certain humming in
this city releases primal forces for those who toil or play until dawn,
while the mortal populace dreams.

Sleep? How could one sleep in this city? It's too vibrant, can't be
leashed, tamed into unconsciousness. One must ride it like a wild tiger,
close to the fur and hungry.

Then one always returns to one's lair, the necessary distractions fading,

****

Mine Okubo was a Japanese American painter who was best known for her
book, *Citizen 13660*, which documented day to day life at the concentration
camp in Topaz, Utah during World War II, with 206 inked line drawings by Mine
and a narrative in her own words. Cameras were not allowed into the camps.
First published in 1946 by Columbia University Press, New York, *Citizen 13660*
remains in print, published by Washington University Press, Washington.

OUTSIDE OF MY WINDOW   *circa 1982*

outside of my window
homeless men and women
chant litanies at dawn
howling   souls raw
lost tempo   oftentimes
strewn in night wake
like so many
broken dolls
on houston and bowery
stoking trashcan fires
hearths against
rain, sleet, snow
I walk by
eyes on the ground

grandmothers lean
elbows upon window ledges
streets below livid with life
neighbors in front of bodegas
drink beer and hold babies
talk of puerto rico
factory-weary lives
maybe better manana
I sidestep cracks and shards of glass

in tompkins square park
kids throw hoops
and make eyes with one another
boomboxes blast disco/rap songs
a joint luminescent
as sun sets into dusk

I take comfort   there are dreams
where I live on the lower east side
loisaida
piecing together
fragments of a life
continue day-to-day

soothed by dreams
searching for that part of my being
whose language and music
cannot be bought
or sold.

A BIG ROUND KITCHEN TABLE

When I was younger, before my father and brother came down with cancer and I had to take care of them, I always imagined having a wonderful, loving partner and we would have five or six children.

I saw a very large kitchen in a simple loft in early Soho, rather than the house in the suburbs, with a big round wooden table with children and their friends gathered around it drawing, working on homework or mixing bubbling science projects together.

Friends and relatives coming and going bringing in news and gossip, sitting for awhile and catching up with a cup of tea or coffee.

On the stove, maybe a big pot of soup or stew is simmering.

Feel the warm sunlight flooding in from white lace curtained windows.

I'm kneading bread or making one of my gigantic salads and all free hands are helping, peeling, busily chopping fresh vegetables gathered from the morning farmers' market.

A tug on my shirt or touch to the elbow and I'm bent over tying a child's shoelace, bandaging a knee or administering first-aid to one of many numerous hamsters, turtles, guinea pigs, cats ...a veritable food chain of pets!

Of course, there under the table, under foot are two golden retrievers or labs with their wagging tails and friendly smiles.

And in a nearby room there is music, someone practicing piano, playing guitar or humming a wordless tune.

MAGIC

For Xian, Dakota, Sydelle, Karlie, Miwa and Maung Gyi

When you were young, you grounded me with the way you saw life: fresh and brilliantly alive; always with a "Why not?" on the tips of your tongues which made me stop and think, "Yes, why not!"

You shared fantastical and wild stories into kingdoms beyond, especially where there were princesses wearing beautiful gowns and pots filled with golden coins and precious jewels. You said, "Auntie! I want Spiderman sneakers!"

You lightened my spirit with your hugs and gifts of drawings and pottery projects, your poetry, the make-believe plays and always the dancing and off-key singing.

You believed you had the power to do anything, be anyone like the Mutant Ninja Turtles or Xena, Warrior Princess and especially on Halloween with your magical wands and silver wings of aluminum foil, and always the glitter, "Don't forget the glitter!", that helped you bring home ten pounds of candy apiece with change to spare.

You showed me practicality and shrewdness in business when you ran yard sales in front of the building hawking old toys and jewelry and books; offered to make pet portraits for a fee or wash the neighbors' pets, promising customers you would study hard and finish school and go to college.

You taught me to look at the world closely, to pay attention to little things like buttercups and their golden powder upon the chin, dune peas' flowers, how to hunt and skin a partridge, read animal tracks, row across the windblown lake surface, to look for eagles nests atop towering birch trees or listen for the call of loons, wonder at spiders and their webs, ants in their colonies, watch worms crawl after a summer rain, use blades of grass for whistling, gaze at butterflies' patterns and colors; to big things like the heavens and the planets Venus or Mars, the Big and Little Dippers there beyond the universe, and to wonder if infinity was a circle.

You kept me on my toes, finding sources of energy I did not know I possessed because you depended upon me to get you where you needed to be, but could not go alone...school, karate, gymnastics, ice skating, swimming, bicycling, art classes, libraries, museums, movies, plays and performances, hiking country, beach and mountains in all seasons... and then when you were older, to watch as you moved boldly into the world.

You showed me kindness and patience beyond your years. "Maybe a cup of tea, but no coffee which is bad for you!" or "Oh don't worry, we can clean up this apartment!" or "Rest now, we can make dinner...how about macaroni and cheese?!"

You forced my mind—oh, tired mind!— to think bigger thoughts, to stay hungry and curious, to dream. You forced me to grow and to move into the future fearlessly or with less fear. And you made my life richer, because of your magic.

CANYON DE CHELLY

For Cathy, Viki, Teru, Clare and Helen

Soundless save the wind
  a raven on the wing
tsegi, rock formations,
    rise magnificently
      from the canyon floor.

Descending switchbacks
  on the White House Trail
    we meet
  a woman scouting a spot
    for her elderly mother's birthday:

My family's from here.
  Mom moved to Chinle town
    and the family comes home
      for celebrations.

She tells us she is on furlough,
  a monthly forced day-off
because of state government
    budget cuts.

Where you from? What do you do?

My friend is an ER doctor
  at the local native hospital
    in Crown Point and
  I work at Project Reach, a youth center in
    New York City's Chinatown
      and Lower East Side.

Our young people have it the worst:
  bad schools, no books and supplies;
  no jobs, nothing to do.
 What's feeding their minds?
 Having kids too early,

lots of drinking
and now crystal meth
    they can make themselves;
violence, depression, suicide.

And you know they're good kids!

Slaughter, starvation,
    centuries of genocide.
They robbed our land. Now they're
    robbing our young, our future.

Look around here:
    no transportation, no roads,
    no water, got to buy water,
    no way out.

    Things have to change
        for our native people.

    I'm hoping they will.

Let me check out the
    trail and make sure it's
    not too slippery for Mom.

    Have a good day now and
        watch out for the heat!

Along the stream
    along the canyon floor
next to the White House ruins
a stand of cottonwoods gives shade
    to native artisans
selling jewelry to tourists
    periodically arriving by jeep

The day before
    at the Hubbell Trading Post
    a guide tells us his story:

When I was 7 years old
    I was taken to an
    Indian Boarding School
        in Oregon, faraway from
            Arizona; it was like the moon
                to a little kid.
    We were forced to forget our
            native languages and customs—
                even our names—
    only to speak English and
        observe the church holidays,
            and ways of white people.
When I was older I came home
    for the summer harvest;
    then when I finished at the
    Boarding School I went
        to college in California,
            but the Vietnam war
            caught up with me.
    Lost a lot of my buddies: Native,
        Black, White, Asian, Chicanos
        all blown to bits.
            I survived.
    In '71, I came home to Chinle,
        joined the National Park Service
        and been a guide since.

I know these Four Corners
    like the back of my hand.
    Been documenting our rock
        paintings in caves, some
            caves that have never been visited
                by folks since those drawings
                    were first made.
    Started by drawing them;
        then by taking photos. Imagine
        carrying all that equipment
            backpacking! And what
            a mess developing them in
            the darkroom with chemicals

                smelling like rotten eggs.
            But I like it best now
                    with these new digital cameras!"
                We laugh.

He tells us how
    the Dineh/Navajo people settled
        these canyons.
    You know, we are related. Native and
        Asians are related.
    We walked across the
            Bering Strait from Asia
                when the land was connected.

Abruptly he asks,
    How do you say "Hello"?
I say, *In Chinese we don't*
    say "Hello" but
    "Nei ho ma", in Cantonese
    meaning, "How are you?"
Startled he says, *In Hopi,*
    we say "Nahoma."
Then he asks, *How about "sit down".*
I say, *Tswo dai.*
He says, *Tst doh.*

We smile like long lost cousins.

Hiking up along the trail
    I run headlong into
    a grandmother/elder sprinting
    down. About four feet ten,
    wiry and spry, dressed in
    traditional vest, long sleeved
    white shirt, an embroidered skirt,
    turquoise and silver jewelry,
    she wears white running shoes and
    has a Nike bag on her back.
I later learn she is 88 years old,
putting my tentative hiking
    to shame!

She asks,
  Where you from?
I say, *From New York City.*
  Where you from?
Down there, first hogan
  on the right.
We eye each other,
    then smile.
      Hot day today. I have
      a lot to do. 'Bye now.
  And turning she says,
    Watch out for that sun!

That night
lying under the stars,
under a cottonwood tree,
the moon rising in an arc,
I know there is something
to be done about
this state of apartheid
in my country.

TALISMANS

You write,
        I've been wearing the jade piece
            you gave me
      with the arrow heads,
          the ox, the wheel,
             and the eternal knot.
      I'm making a more elaborate
          necklace to hang it on,
               but for now it's on a length of
                   golden embroidery floss

I write,
        the soapstone medallion
          you gave me,
      with a flower carved lightly
          in its center,
          is safely pinned within
             my woven Tibetan bag tied to
               golden embroidery floss

     Reminders of a summer past
      we howled with laughter
      under a rising moon
        the milky way
      heavenly skies
        laced with glittering
        stars and constellations
    woods and streams we trekked
        bedecked in wild
        grass and flowery crowns;
    made drawings with
        found charcoal on flat rocks,
        we placed upon a cairn—

          an offering

        from two time-travelers
          whose spirits
            cross paths
             with ease

LANDSCAPE

Clouds ear
   lotus root
      bamboo
      shitake
         soy bean
      swirling in "don fa"
         egg flower
      ingredients for
         hot and sour soup

      A dollar container
         in Chinatown
           brings me home
           to a landscape
              lost long ago

HOME

Gingko trees in bud on 4th street
      are silhouettes dark
         against twilit blue skies
      are brush strokes in Chinese landscapes
         "shan/shwei hwar"
         mountain/water paintings
      are yearnings for China
           my ancestral home

Here, in the East Village
      there is such tenderness
         in this evening's
           spring air

MI GATO PEQUEÑO

From Peru you call excitedly,
    I'm in the Sacred Valley
      an hour from Cuzco
        in the Andes Mountains
        in the loft of an old barn and
    the family who owns the land
     charges ten dollars a month and
       insisted I pay only half
       since I'll only be here for two weeks.
    They are so kind, but I insisted,
      "No, I couldn't do that!" and
      paid in full. We smile across many miles
         over that.

The village grocer and his family
    lets me cook breakfast on their stove
    the eggs, cheese I purchase every day
    with tomatoes and apples and bread.
    Twice a day the family makes
    large pots of fresh food they sell
    by the heaping platefuls for lunch and dinner.
    Travelers in town and apprentices
    from around the world
    studying at the French hippie clown
    commune school across the road
    gather together to eat and there's always
    music and juggling and singing!

Hiking through green mountains,
    ripening cornfields
    to nearby ruins, pass
     pristine springs, the sun
     golden and blue skies filled
     with billowing clouds and when
     the mist rises it is so beautiful—
     someday, we must see this
     together, Mama.

SEVEN CONTINENTS, NINE LIVES

And why shouldn't the world
   call to us
  the seven continents
    that's spun before us
     from the painted metal globes
      of our childhoods:
         oceans and seas,
         mountains and deserts
         great and small
         and all that is in between
         north and south
         poles, ice and snow-laden.

Beckoning us
  beyond familiar ground
   beyond familiar selves
   meeting head-on
   people and cultures
   forcing us to open our
      hearts, minds, souls
      moving from one life to the next
        like cats with nine lives

      Now. In the present.
     In this life.
       In this one life.

Fay Chiang is a writer, artist and community/cultural activist living and working in Chinatown and the Lower East Side of New York City for the past four decades. Raised in the backroom of a laundry in Queens by immigrant parents from Guandong, China, she writes from her experiences as a woman of color from the working class. She believes culture is a psychological weapon to reclaim our past, define our present and to envision possibilities for our future; that the development of culture is an integral part of progressive social change and social justice movements. Currently working at Project Reach, a youth and community center for young people at risk in Chinatown/Lower East Side, she lives in the East Village and sees many journeys with her daughter, Xian.

Ding Kong is a young educator/artist/activist teaching 7th grade math/science in Downtown Los Angeles. Born and raised in China for 8 years, emigrated to Germany for 2 years; he then immigrated to Los Angeles with his family. His artistic and pedagogical practices are heavily influenced by Paolo Freire, bell hooks, Gloria Anzaldua, and Vijay Prashad; and by his work experience at Project Reach in New York City.

ABOUT THE AUTHOR *(Editor's Note)*

Fay Chiang's work is complex. Born of anger, it is ultimately optimistic about the importance of the artist as a preserver and perpetuator of culture, and of the self-determination of the individual in a society in which pressures to conform persist. Her unflinching sense of fairness and justice and her intolerance of hypocrisy seem at odds with her *joie de vivre* and good humor. In truth, her tenacity and clear vision are the strength of her work, both artistic and political.

Fay Chiang grew up in Queens in the 1950s, in a section formerly called Jackson Heights (now East Elmhurst); one of three Chinese-American families in the neighborhood.

Chiang's father had come over from China in the 1930s as a "paper son"; he lived in the back of a laundry with an older brother, and as a teenager himself began working in a laundry. After the war, he returned to China to meet a prospective bride, Fay's mother. Chiang recalls her mother being "just furious" at being married off to a virtual stranger after only meeting briefly. Though her parents were from well-to-do families in China and were landowners with servants, as immigrants, their life in the United States was one of hard work. They established a shirt-pressing factory in New York, which failed. For a brief period, Fay and her mother and baby sister lived in the family tenement apartment on Bayard Street in New York's Chinatown while her father set up the laundry in Queens.

Fay and her two sisters and brother lived with their parents in the back of the laundry. She recalls feeling angry at the segregation at that time; although she had many friends at school, she was rarely invited into their homes, and as one of few Asian American families in the neighborhood, felt she didn't fit in at school or even at church.

As a high school student, Chiang studied Mandarin at Columbia. In her senior year she applied and was accepted into the School of Visual Arts, Pratt Institute and the Fashion Institute of Technology and awarded partial scholarships. She was unable to attend because her parents would not give her their income tax forms to apply for financial aid. Her mother said if she attended Barnard College, assuring she would meet a future Chinese American Columbia University husband, the family would pay tuition but not for art school.

Instead she attended tuition-free Hunter College, where she majored in fine arts. It was there that Chiang became active in the anti-war movement, first through the mostly-white Student Mobilization Committee, and later with Asian Americans Against the War (AAA) a group led by Japanese American women (Yuri Kochiyama, Min Matsuda and Cazu Iijima) who had been incarcerated in concentrations camps during World War Two. This group encouraged the younger generation to become active as Asian Americans with their own agenda against the war by questioning, "Why should Asians be killing other Asians?"

Chiang also was a pioneer in the movement to create Asian American studies programs within the City University system. Working with Professor C T Wu, the author of *Chink*, which was an anthology of anti-Chinese American legislation, Fay with other Asian American students and allies sought each semester to get enough signatures on petitions to maintain an Asian American studies course, and negotiated to find departments to sponsor it. She joined the college's Chinese Club, then primarily a social organization, and was elected secretary and later president. As president, she changed the name of the club to ASIA, Asian Students In Action, and the agenda from socializing to include activities that built awareness on Asian American identity, history and issues affecting Asian American communities socially and politically, becoming active in the faculty and student government on the curriculum committee, and in the student government on the finance committees. Forging coalitions from the Student Mobilization Committee with the Black and Puerto Rican Studies Department, Women's Studies and Gay and Lesbian groups on campus and in Hunter's Student Government, Fay and other students gained the support to establish the Asian American History and Identity course at Hunter. She developed the curriculum for the course in a field with little literature by cobbling together guest speakers for transmission of oral history with the literature that did exist. As a college sophomore in 1970, Fay Chiang, under the auspices of Professor Wu, taught the course that she and her group had worked to establish and fund.

Through her involvement with the Asian American Anti-War movement, Chickens Come Home To Roost (anti-gentrification on the Upper West Side) and meeting other students setting up Asian American studies courses and programs at City College, Queens College, Lehman College and Columbia University, Fay was introduced to the Basement Workshop in the Spring of 1971. A fledgling non-profit organization in a small basement of a tenement building at 54 Elizabeth Street, Basement Workshop was founded by Danny Yung of Columbia University's Urban Studies Department and Frank Ching and Margaret Lo of the New York Times, Peter Pan, Chi Wing Ho and Eleanor Yung. They had recently published the inaugural issue of Bridge Magazine, a bimonthly covering Asian American issues and culture.

Having completed the Chinatown Report of 1969, the first census of Chinatown community residents, funded by the Ford Foundation, Danny's idea was to use the information gathered as a basis to start the Asian American Resource Center and to begin collecting resources, artifacts and oral histories of the aging community residents of the Bachelor Society. He conceived Basement Workshop as an umbrella that would incubate projects and programs that would eventually become separate and independent entities.

Fay Chiang left after her initial visit to the Basement Workshop having decided to return in the fall, after a planned trip to Hong Kong and Taiwan, where she was to study Mandarin. The trip in 1971 was to be formative in terms of her defining her self as an American and to begin the journey to define a life, work and a place in this society. In Hong Kong she became acquainted with the different sectors of her family, some quite wealthy, others living in rooftop shacks or in a loft where they also knitted sweaters for a living. In this way, she was confronted with issues of class, and forced to consider them.

Afterward, she journeyed to California, where she became acquainted with Chinese, Japanese and Filipino Americans who were setting up Asian American Studies programs and departments at UCLA, UC Berkeley, UC Davis, and San Francisco State University where she collected curricula for the Asian American studies programs in NYC. She also visited community-based organizations such as Kearny Street Workshop, Japanese American Media Workshop and the "I" Hotel in San Francisco; and Amerasia Books, the Pioneer Community Senior Center, Gidra, Visual Communications and Yellow Brotherhood in Los Angeles. The journey was instrumental in Chiang's decision to return and work in the New York City Asian American community.

Chiang became more involved with the Basement Workshop in the Fall of 1971. She worked on Yellow Pearl and Bridge Magazine, and in January of 1973, became coordinator of Amerasia Creative Arts. However, in the fall of 1972, Chiang's father developed cancer; as eldest daughter, it was Fay's role to become his caregiver. Fay left Hunter, devoting her time to Basement and her family. (She ultimately received a Bachelor of Arts degree from the School of Visual Arts in New York City). At this time, she also shifted away from doing art and began writing.

At that time, political factions in Chinatown were primarily informed by the politics in China. Chiang's interest was in the Asian experience in America based on the lives of a new generation of children of immigrants, through shifts in class, economic and educational status. She and her Yellow Pearl cohorts considered it their mandate to write about their own communities, to talk about their own experience, and to create and develop their own culture. This form of activism often came into conflict with the desires of those who wanted to use the Basement Workshop as a political organizing space, while Chiang felt that developing a community's culture was a form of social and political change, that is, cultural activism was a means to individual and collective psychological survival.

Chiang became executive director of the Basement Workshop in 1974, and was involved with the organization through 1986; she also served as the director of Henry Street Settlement's Asian American Outreach Program, project manager and special sections editor in New York Newsday's Public Affairs Office, and director of Poets & Writers Readings/Workshops state-wide re-grant program. Fay joined Project Reach in 2000 as its program/development director and a crisis counselor for young people at risk.

Fay has served and continues to work as a volunteer for the Ad Hoc Committee, The Orchard Street Advocacy and Drop In Center, October 22nd Coalition Against Police Brutality; and as a board member of Dramatic Risks, Border Statements, and When I Walk. She was also a member of the Feminist Writers Guild and Kitchen Table Press.

In addition to her two previous volumes of poetry, *In The City of Contradictions* (Sunbury Press 1979) and *Miwa's Song* (Sunbury 1982), Fay Chiang's poetry and prose has been published in anthologies, including the landmark Ordinary Women (1978), *Voci Dal Silenzio* (I Canguri/Feltrinelli, Milan), *Changer L'Amerique: Anthologie de la Protestaire USA* (La Maison de la Poesie, Rhones-Alps), *Breaking Silence (Greenfield Review Press, NY), Girls: An Anthology* (Global City Press), *Quiet Fire* (Asian American Writers Workshop, NY), *American Born and Foreign* (Sunbury Press, NY), and *Bowery Women: Poems* (Bowery Books 2006), and in journals, such as *Amerasia Journal, Tribes Magazine*, and *The Mom Egg*.

A recipient of a New York State CAPS Poetry grant, a Revson Fellowship at Columbia University, Lifetime Achievement Awards from New York University's Asian/Pacific American Studies Department (NYU/APA) and the Writers Voice Award from the Five Colleges, Massachusetts, Fay has taught poetry, visual arts and playwriting as an artist in residence in venues such as the 63rd Street Y's Writers Voice, Plays for Living, Project Reach, Art in General and Dramatic Risks, and at NYU/APA. She was a visiting scholar under the auspices of NYU/APA's program.

Current projects include a memoir, her book-length poem "Chinatown, and another book-length poetry manuscript, "In This Life". The latter is based on her conversations as a breast cancer survivor with a friend living with AIDS. She has compiled archival recordings of her work and life experiences with Jack Tchen and Jason Hwang at NYU/APA; will complete shooting and co-editing a documentary of API people living with HIV/AIDS in NYC with Siddhartha Joag; is producing a documentary "Do What You Got To Do", directed by Mark Waren, on the history of Joe Cino and the advent of the Off-Off Broadway theater movement and The Café Cino; and has done staged readings of her play, *Two Boots and A Ball Gown* with Mary Lum and Regie Cabico. Going back to her roots as a visual artist, she continues a series of portrait paintings and drawings of friends and people from the many cross communities, among them October 22nd Against Police Brutality's youth who have been killed by the NYPD. She is also involved with Zero Capital (www.zerocapital.net), an intergenerational artists' and activists' collective dedicated to facilitating the making and exhibiting of art for social change outside of the commercial mainstream; as well as the Pine Ridge Project which is linking native schools on reservations across the United States with public and private schools in New York City in an exchange of school and art supplies and students' life experiences; and the Basement Workshop Documentation Project at NYU's APA studies program culminating in an updated Basement Workshop Yearbook/Reader of essays, visual arts, oral histories, photographs, music lyrics and artifacts archived in NYU's permanent library collection.

Fay Chiang resides in New York's East Village; and is mother to Xian. In a 2003 interview, Fay Chiang spoke of the importance of owning your own life, allowing yourself the freedom to discover what you want to put your time and energy into regardless of familial and societal pressures; and how the clarity of one's life choices leads to personal as well as social change and activism. And despite prejudice, family tragedies, and personal health problems, she has done just that.

7 Continents 9 Lives includes selections from Chiang's two previous books of poetry and a generous helping of new work.

In *In The City of Contradictions* (originally edited and published by Virginia Scott of Sunbury Press in 1979), Chiang recounts her journey, as an artist, writer, and activist, from her family's sparely furnished room behind the laundry in Queens, to the anti-war demonstrations of college in the 70s, to dreaming and making dreams a reality on the Lower East Side. *Miwa's Song* (also edited and published by Virginia Scott of Sunbury Press, 1982) begins with a parable about a little girl and a globe, and goes on to relate Fay's journeys in Mexico. Her newer work, *Midnight Blue Sky,* expands on these themes, while also exploring her experiences as an activist working with young people at risk (immigrant, undocumented, LGBT, homeless, suicide, domestic violence, rape, teen parenthood) and people living with HIV/AIDS and chronic illnesses such as cancer and multiple sclerosis in New York City, and her experiences as a parent.

Chiang has the instincts and attention to nuance of a traveler, whether discussing a foreign country or her own Lower East Side, or the streets of her memories, or those of her forebears. It is as if her experience as the child of immigrants has given her a permanent lens through which to view her experiences with the dispassionate eyes of the "Other". In chronicling racism, sexism, homophobia,

149

class prejudice and hypocrisy, Chiang is unflinching in her assessments of our society, but always with an attitude of compassion, which admits to the possibility of change. Her approach appears to be similar to the way which she viewed her own poverty, a pragmatic optimism ("we've got two hands apiece, we'll figure something out"), an attitude which she also employs to cope with unrelenting attacks of cancer upon her family and person; Chiang has had seven operations in 12 years.

Her view of beauty is equally clear-eyed, understated, and unsentimental. In "Home," she notices, "Here, in the East Village/there is such tenderness/in this evening's/spring air". Chiang is alive to the particulars, whether she is discussing her beloved Lower East Side, the daily routines of an elderly widow in Italy or a family in Peru, or the final days of an AIDS patient whom she accompanied to hospice. To Fay Chiang, love is in the details, the personal is political, the elements of culture live in their transmission as art and life.

–Marjorie Tesser

The following articles were sources for some of the information in this essay:
"Interview with Fay Chiang" by Jennifer Tan, Staff Writer, *Generasian* Spring 03 http://www.nyu.edu/clubs/generasian/spring03/Features/faychiang.htm

"On Art and Institution: Fay Chiang at Eth-Noh-Tec, SF, 2009 MARCH 14" by Barbara Jane Reyes http://bjanepr.wordpress.com/2009/03/14/on-art-and-institution-fay-chiang-at-eth-noh-tec-sf/
"Fay Chiang" by Mia Kang, Nodutdol E News, March 2009, http://nodutdol.org

CPSIA information can be obtained
at www.ICGtesting.com
Printed in the USA
LVHW02s1747131117
556112LV00005B/463/P